# DEATH FROM THE SEA

## BY THE SAME AUTHOR

THE LAFAYETTE ESCADRILLE
HIGH FLEW THE FALCONS
BOLD MEN, FAR HORIZONS
THE NEW TIGERS
THE GREAT PURSUIT

*For younger readers:*

FAMOUS FIRSTS IN EXPLORATION
THE COMMANDOS
THE TEXAS RANGERS
DUEL FOR THE SKY

# DEATH
# from the Sea

OUR GREATEST NATURAL DISASTER
THE GALVESTON HURRICANE OF 1900

## HERBERT MOLLOY MASON, JR.

 THE DIAL PRESS
NEW YORK 1972

Library of Congress Cataloging in Publication Data

Mason, Herbert Molloy.
  Death from the sea.

  SUMMARY:   A description, based on survivors' accounts
and official records, of the hurricane and flood that
devastated the island city of Galveston in September,
1900.
  Bibliography:  p.
  1. Galveston—Storm, 1900—Juvenile literature.
  [1. Galveston—Storm, 1900.   2.   Hurricanes]
I.   Title.
F394.G2M3        976.4′139        70—37445

PRINTED IN THE UNITED STATES OF AMERICA
FIRST PRINTING 1972

DESIGNED BY JOEL SCHICK

Warmest climes but nurse the cruelest fangs: the tiger of Bengal crouches in spiced groves of ceaseless verdure. Skies the most effulgent but basket the deadliest thunders: gorgeous Cuba knows tornadoes that never swept tamer lands . . . the Typhoon will sometimes burst from out of that cloudless sky, like an exploding bomb upon a dazed and sleepy town.

—HERMAN MELVILLE
*Moby Dick*

# CONTENTS

# DEATH FROM THE SEA

# Chapter 1

## THE KILLER BORN

I N LATE SUMMER the sun beats hard against the empty green seas of the central Atlantic. Thin clouds begin to erase themselves as soon as the rim of the sun splits the horizon. Clean and brassy skies beckon sea birds to flight through shining air. Rising currents loft them in effortless sweeps in the constant search for nourishment from the sea; at first high in vigilant reconnaissance for telltale silver flashes of schools of fish on the move, then sliding down to skim the ocean's roof, slender wings and feathered plumpness buoyed by the cushion of warm air pressing upward in gentle persuasion.

But the rising air that makes flight for these wanderers so shamelessly easy breeds destruction for uncounted thousands of aerial migrants caught in unfortunate passage across the Tropic of Cancer during the month of the tern.

It was a time of parched skies, and after long weeks of absorbing brutal heat from an unshielded sun, bleak acres of ocean offered the atmosphere a womb for the quick gestation of disaster. Late in August, 1900, in a trackless area along the parallel more than a thousand miles west of Dakar, the ocean began to heave in anger. The air, thickened with radiant heat, roiled upward laden with moisture; the sea, rebelling against the ruthless sun, was reacting with turbulent bursts of perspiration. The rapid ascent of heated air masses caused large areas of unequal pressure to form near the surface of the sea. Denser air rushed in to fill the thinner pockets, creating erratic winds across a sprawling expanse and accelerating the uprush of air in its convective escape from the valleys of the Atlantic. Tenuous clouds formed, growing fat with moisture as they raced upward to lofty altitudes, casting dark shadows on the disturbed seas thousands of feet below.

The turbulence was embedded in the easterly trade-wind belt sprawling across the tropics, reaching from the sea to heights of seven miles and more, moving sluggishly toward the Caribbean and its multitude of islands.

Not yet a storm, the "easterly wave" was a low-pressure trough riding along with the prevailing current. Stabilized, the wave could have traveled for thousands of miles with little change, but the great convective forces already at work coupled with convergence of flowing air masses that surrounded it created an imbalance within the system, and as the wave moved slowly across the Atlantic its character became less benign. Massive cumulus and cumulonimbus clouds rose from an increasing humidness, vaulting into vast and dark cathedrals. The sky rumbled and boomed with a cannonade of thunder. The wave, already accelerating vertically, was forced into a broad counterclockwise spiral by the rotation of the earth. The wave, once a docile passenger within the easterly trades, now pressured the air around it to curl in upon itself. With the passage of hours during the day and the night the great spiral arms of the embryonic storm began tightening into a cyclonic corkscrew.

Atmospheric pressure at the bottom of the newly created vortex dropped rapidly, forming a hollow eye of relative calm at the center of the surrounding tumult. Heavier air outside the system swept in to fill the void, tending to fill the core and so cause the storm to collapse upon itself and die. But the cold prevailing winds aloft swept across the crown of the storm, pumping these fresh inputs of air out like smoke boiling up a flue. Water vapor inside the spiraling arms condensed, releasing enormous amounts of heat energy that added fresh violence to the twisting forces already at work. Thus was created an awesome heat engine feeding upon the atmosphere around it.

Within seventy-two hours the storm stood as a dervish perhaps two miles high and spreading across as much as a hundred miles of the Atlantic. It swelled itself with fury and began its inexorable march westward.

The greatest travelers of them all, the slender arctic terns, poured by the thousands across the Tropic of Cancer, near the half-way mark of an annual ten-thousand-mile migratory journey to Antarctica, and plunged into an alien atmosphere. The unblemished air through which they had been flying turned thick and heavy. The brilliant sun, the terns' navigational aid since the dawn of time, vanished in a yellow iridescent haze. The flocks of swift birds bored on until they reached the storm's ragged edge. Violent winds frustrated their passage, scattered their formations and battered individual birds senseless. Many of the terns managed successfully to ride the winds on the skirts of the system, not fighting it, but moving with it, and reached the white world of the Antarctic many weeks late after being blown as much as two thousand miles off course.

The storm's cyclonic spiral was marked by heavy cloud bands gushing torrential rains, separated by areas of light rain or no rain at all. Lightning cracked and roared through these bands, stabbing out in every direction. Many of the birds were drawn helplessly into the vortex and torn apart. Still others somehow made it through the shifting layers of screaming winds to reach the unearthly silence of the eye where they fluttered down to crash exhausted into the sea.

By August 30 the periphery of the storm was less than six hundred miles east southeast of Puerto Rico, and sailors aboard ships nearing the 60th meridian, bound for nearby Guadeloupe or Martinique, were the first men to feel the effects of the onrushing tropical fury. These seamen cursed the oppressive air around them that was suffocating in its stillness. Deck hands sprawled in whatever shade they could find; bare metal plating exposed for days to the sun was too hot to lay bare skin to. Below, engine-room gangs gushed sweat and oil, sweltering in 120-degree temperatures. Topside ventilators were turned this way and that, seeking vestiges of a breeze to channel belowdecks, but the effort was futile; there was no breeze. Smoke struggled with difficulty out of funnels, and instead of streaming away in a graceful plume it spread and flattened like an evil cloud and rained soot on the decks. The sun paled, casting sickly shadows. Sailors complained of the sulphurous air, saying it smelled of rotten eggs.

Old hands read the ominous signs, predicting fearful weather ahead—a forecast buttressed when the sun disappeared in an incarnadine sky.

Ships caught up in the great swells sent rolling in the vanguard of the storm wallowed in dark troughs. Sweating crewmen in the fo'c'sle, wrapped like larvae in canvas cocoons, swung heavily back and forth with each creaking roll. In galleys, ladles and pots banged with metronomic clatter. The first large cold drops of rain pelted down, coming at first in an erratic drumming, then in blinding torrents to merge with black seas crashing against hulls, seemingly from every direction. Ships were swallowed in the howling maelstrom and began fighting for survival.

Once generated, nothing stood in the way of the great storm in its steady drift across the Atlantic and into the Caribbean. Tropical storms do not form over water much below 80 degrees Fahrenheit, nor can they survive over cooler waters, for it is the temperature difference between air and water that drives and sustains the complex makeup of the system. Decreases in water temperature, which rob a storm of its heat source, are almost nonexistent along the hurricane latitudes from August to November. No friction-inducing land masses stand in the way of tropical disturbances born in the far eastern Atlantic. Had geological evolution placed a small continent in the central Atlantic, roughly between the latitudes of northern Florida and the Panama Canal, most tropical storms would be drained of their energy before maturing as full-blown hurricanes. But this storm, like hundreds before it, fed itself and grew in fury for three thousand miles before bulling its way toward Hispaniola, a slender barrier at best.

Forty-eight hours before the first winds struck Dominican fishermen plying their *feluccas* in the Mona Passage between Cape Egaño and Isla Saona were already reading the signs foretelling foul weather ahead; their boats were rocked by long, low swells rolling in from east-southeast—swells stronger than the usual trade-wind sort and coming from a slightly different direction. Inland, sugarcane and sisal plantation workers suffered under a blazing sky devoid of the promise of cooling showers. There were only a few fair-weather cumuli far off in the distance, and these could do no good. The friendly trade winds had lost their refreshing punch, dropping to a halfhearted intensity barely moving the palm fronds. Soon there were no winds at all and the sea and the land lay baking in an atmospheric oven.

Late in the afternoon fitful warm breezes arose, erratic in direction, and along the distant horizon ice-crystal wisps of cirrus clouds formed, beautiful in their shining, ranked structure—but dangerous omens, for they were formed by condensing water vapor swept out of the core of the storm, the spiral bands of cumulonimbus having reached the convective limits of cloud formation.

The fishermen dragged their boats ashore and pegged them to earth. Smooth clouds obscured the sun and gusting winds tore among the trees, ripping away fronds in 30-m.p.h. bursts. Swells rolled in to the beaches in a foaming barrage. Nails were found and shutters were boarded tight. Children, pigs and chickens were hopefully sealed inside shacks, and the islanders fatalistically awaited the coming of the *hura-*

*cán*, named after the Quiché god of thunder and lightning and evil winds.

Fortunately for the islanders, the storm, although larger than the island itself, was not yet fully grown, nor did its center carve a path down the ridge of low mountains that forms the spine of both the Dominican Republic and Haiti. The center of violence was a hundred miles out to sea when the northeast quadrant blew ashore near Santo Domingo on the morning of September 1, bringing strong winds howling through the city, winds strong enough to bend trees, to rattle houses, and to make walking in any direction except leeward a difficult challenge. Heavy rains, coming in squalls, drummed against tin roofs and spurted into the crooked streets, turning them into rivers and quick-running muddy gruel. While Santo Domingo was still being whipped and drenched by the aft quadrant of the storm, the forward edges reached out for Port-au-Prince, 130 miles further on, departing there on September 2 to leap the Windward Passage separating Haiti from Cuba. The stretch of water between Port-au-Prince and Santiago measures 250 miles, a distance the storm covered in twelve hours, picking up new energy from the sea as it went.

The storm dumped 16.56 inches of rain on Santiago within less than twenty-four hours, a statistic that could have meant pestilential disaster a year earlier. Cubans, under four hundred years of Spanish rule, had never known a system of underground drainage. Commenting on conditions in Cuban cities just prior to the Spanish-American War, author and correspondent José de Olivares observed:

"So vile is the bed of the harbor that it is the custom of

ships upon leaving to deodorize and disinfect their anchors, for germs of all manner of deadly diseases lurk in the filth of ages that adheres to their flukes. When a gale blows from the harbor toward the city the foul waters of the bay are driven out and inundate several of the adjacent streets, depositing the seeds of disease and death and leaving a ghastly smell that only the educated olfactory can endure.

"Some of the streets are paved with stone, while others are merely dirt roads which become impassable in wet weather. The streets are very narrow, with sidewalks not more than two feet wide, and in many instances these are entirely lacking. These old streets have no gutters, but usually decline slightly from both sides toward the center, where the filth collects and decays or is washed off by the rains. Dead cats, dogs and other small animals are left in the streets for days, while in poorer localities slops, night soil and filth are thrown out of doors and windows of the houses and find a common receptacle in the middle of the street."

Under the administration of Major General Leonard Wood, the Corps of Engineers sanitized the harbors of Santiago and Havana and had largely completed underground drainage systems in both cities by the time the storm drenched the island. Santiago's conduit-like, twisting, plunging streets became spirited and uncontrollable rivers from the tons of water that poured from the sky and swept down from nearby hills, but the Engineers' subterranean pipes held and a major epidemic was averted.

Tropical storms are vagrant in character and irrational in movement; no two have ever traced an identical Caribbean passage, and directional trends of these storms are so broad as to be virtually meaningless to even the most skilled observers trying to guess which turn the storm will take next. Providentially, there is no guarantee that tropical disturbances that develop into true storms will ever reach land; about 75 percent of such storms born at sea die at sea. Studies over an eighty-year span show that an average of eight tropical cyclones and five true hurricanes will develop and mature in the Atlantic during the season that begins in June and ends in November—and those born in August live the longest and are often the most dangerous.

Great storms that live long enough do, however, tend to move erratically westward for many days before recurving in parabolas of varying pitch. Thus a storm that reaches Cuba after a week or more of travel might reasonably be expected to shift its line of attack and move against Florida or the Carolinas. And this is what happened.

On September 5, with the storm ten days old, the cyclonic mass jumped clear of Havana harbor after swamping the city and veered north for Key West. The center of the hurricane—for such it now was, with winds exceeding 74 m.p.h. —picked up a new heading of approximately 330 degrees and crossed the 25th parallel. This hurricane, nameless and newly fueled by warm offshore waters, swelled until it measured four hundred miles from one ragged edge to the other, the gyrating arms encompassing more than 150,000 square miles of heavy rains and tearing winds. Larger than the state of New Mexico, larger than the areas of Alabama and Georgia combined, the storm system was too vast for the minds of men unschooled in the forces of nature to envision or to comprehend.

But observers of the youthful Weather Bureau in Washington, D.C. (the agency was barely ten years old) knew full well the potential of disaster that loomed and began issuing special bulletins on the fourth, while the storm was still battering central Cuba. Residents of Tampa were warned of the approaching danger, and many hastily gathered up the essentials of living and fled inland.

The hurricane moved steadily northward for the next twenty-four hours, radiating destruction for hundreds of miles in every direction. On Thursday, September 6, the Mallory Line steamer *Comal*, outbound from New York, battled its way into port at Key West more than forty hours overdue. The captain, a storm-weary man named Evans, explained that his 2251-ton freighter had run afoul of heavy seas, fierce gales and torrential rains upon reaching Jupiter Light off Florida's eastern coast and that he was lucky to have limped into safe harbor at Key West, however late. Evans offloaded cargo and was interviewed by reporters. He told them of ships seen smashed up along the Florida coast. "A bark at Turtle Harbor," Evans recounted, "a four-masted schooner and a barkentine near French Reef, and a square-rigged vessel near Sombrero Light."

Despite the recent buffeting sustained by the *Comal*, Evans stubbornly refused to lay over at Key West until the storm had blown itself out; he was due in Galveston on the eleventh, and the storm had delayed him long enough as it was. Besides, it was clear that the heavy weather was moving due north. On the morning of the seventh, the *Comal* slipped her moorings and set course for Texas, westward across the Gulf of Mexico.

The storm, which until now had earned only cryptic mention on the weather page far in the back of the New York *Times*, jumped to the front page and national attention for the first time on Friday, September 7. Captain Evans's account of his battle to round the Florida bend was given prominence, as was the news that the mayor of Trinidad had wired the military government pleading for help because "the cyclone has destroyed all the crops and the people are destitute." What had been merely another tropical disturbance in the remote Caribbean became overnight a trespasser of frightening proportions threatening to break in the nation's back door.

Sympathetic disturbances spread, and damage and disaster reports flowed from a wide arc. Major eastern dailies flashed ominous headlines:

"STORM NEAR BALTIMORE"

"MANY WRECKS ON FLORIDA COAST"

"JAMAICA SWEPT BY BIG STORM"

"CONSIDERABLE DAMAGE AT WEST PALM BEACH—PIER WASHED AWAY—SEA WALLS DAMAGED—SMALL BOATS SUNK"

In New Orleans, people were driven indoors when winds up to 48 m.p.h. lashed the city, and in Atlanta—250 miles inland from either coast—telephone lines were ripped down by gale winds that battered at the Metaine Bridge until it collapsed and went flying in a debris of splintered wood and filigreed metal. The first loss of life was reported with this line: "A child was killed, being blown together with the entire front balcony from a house on Front Street."

Just when the southern states braced for an ordeal similar to the one of October 1, 1893, that killed more than two thousand people living along the coastal plains of Alabama, Louisiana and Mississippi, reprieve came with dramatic suddenness. On the night of Thursday, September 6, the mammoth hurricane heeled hard around in a 90-degree turn to port, picked up speed, and started churning its way due west across the Gulf of Mexico.

Why had the great storm shifted direction? Where would it strike now? The answers could not be given then, nor can the same questions be answered about these tropical freaks today: hurricanes have no sane helmsmen steering them along a predictable course. Overlays of dozens of tracks of past hurricanes drive home the point that tropical storms seemingly are directed by no natural laws. These tracks, when laid on a map of the West Indies, the Caribbean and the Gulf of Mexico resemble doodlings of the demented. Some start straight north, execute a single large loop in the empty ocean, then die. Some drive for Cuba like an express train, then make a hairpin turn and plunge back to the east. Some strike for Yucatán, then lazily form complete loops and veer to the northeast for a swipe at Louisiana. Others have begun at the top of South America to loop their way north across Cuba and Florida before perversely swinging west to die somewhere over Arkansas.

Hurricanes have a maddening disregard for the orderly syllogistic reasoning process that begins, "If . . . then . . ." To the weathermen watching the radically changing readings given by their instruments measuring atmospheric vagaries, it was a time of intense frustration. All their data, current to the hour, their own experience and the meticulous records kept by those before them were practically useless. While it was true that hurricanes tended to invade nearby low-pressure areas and were sometimes fenced in by neighboring highs, hurricanes had been known to chew their way through such areas of high pressure as though they did not exist. When the hurricane had executed its unexpected turn to the west there was such a barrier of high pressure running along the Gulf coast from Pensacola on past El Paso. Would the hurricane be kept at bay by this high and crash inland south of the Rio Grande? They did not know.

Twenty-four hours passed, and the hurricane remained on course, aimed like an arrow at the "golden coast" of Texas. Hundreds of miles of open, warm water in the path of the storm precluded the possibility that the hurricane might weaken, or die. It was the longest-lived hurricane within recent memory, and even should it turn once again, or even execute a hairpin reverse, there was slight chance it could escape the great, thousand-mile bowl of the Gulf of Mexico before spending its fury somewhere along the populated coastline stretching in a sweeping curve from Yucatán to the southern tip of Florida.

To wish for the storm to veer from its present course of approximately 270 degrees would mean only to wish the visitation of disaster upon one group of people rather than another. Urgent warnings were sent out from Biloxi to Brownsville.

The weathermen could only watch, warn, and wait as the hurricane thrashed its way across the Gulf south of New Orleans. They gave Texas another thirty hours before the hurricane reached the target it had been seeking for nearly four thousand miles.

# Chapter 2

# FAIR ISLE

A S THE SUMMER OF 1900 drew to a close, Galveston was never more beautiful, never more prosperous. Galveston was the largest port in Texas and third largest in the nation in clearing grain for export, nearing 25 million tons of wheat and corn annually for Liverpool, Le Havre, Rotterdam, Manchester, Belfast, Aarhus and a dozen other foreign trade centers. Great coal-burning cargo ships, proud square-rigged barkentines aflight with billowing canvas, and low-lying coastal schooners paraded constantly along the ocean roads leading to Galveston, keeping the miles of wharves filled to capacity. Twelve hundred ships a year on the average entered and cleared with more than $300 million in cargo. Out flowed nearly 70 percent of the nation's cotton export, and grain, flour, breadstuffs, zinc, ore, sawn lumber, cottonseed oil, beef, hogs and dairy products; in came beet sugar, jute butts, sisal, cement, coffee and chemicals.

Three tremendous storage elevators bulging with almost four million bushels of grain loomed over the docks; the vast elongated sheds lining the quays were packed with thousands of bales of new cotton, and smoke plumed from tall chimneys marking the city's many manufacturing compounds: the five-story brewery, the cotton mill, the rope and twine factory, the Texas Star Flour and Rice Mills, the sprawling cottonseed oil processing plant, the baggage and cordage works, and Clarke & Courts, one of the largest printing and stationery firms in America. These were major industrial concerns; the Galveston City Cotton Mill, for example, manufactured more textiles than any plant in Texas, with five hundred workers on the payroll to deal with 20,000 spindles and 590 looms. There were another sixty industries of varying sizes in Galveston, ranging from cotton compresses to a hat and shoe factory.

Feeding, and fed by, these plants were 37,789 people, most of whom claimed that they lived in the finest city in the state, if not along the entire Gulf Coast. Galveston was certainly the most beautiful. True, Dallas, Houston and San Antonio had larger populations—ranging from five thousand more in Dallas to sixteen thousand more in San Antonio— but all three were considered rowdy frontier towns growing haphazardly and lacking in social graces and cultural attainments.

Dallas, booming on the prairie, was a rail crossroads, jammed with wagons and livestock struggling with the city's narrow streets that were quagmires of waxy black mud after sudden rains and maddening thoroughfares choked with orange dust at any other time. The sound of the city was a cacaphonous blend of mooings, bleatings, ear-piercing train whistles, exasperated shouts of wagon drivers and the melodious thump-and-clangor of player pianos issuing from the town's many saloons. These were the sounds of progress in cattle- and cotton-hungry southwestern America, but the price was a strangled, congested city dangerous to navigate because of serpentine streets and an abundance of unguarded rail crossings. With big money coming into town to stay, a few monumental homes were rising from the prairie earth, but they were overwhelmed by the thousands of flat-fronted, flat-roofed frame boxes that were hastily nailed together side by side and occupied anyhow, without regard for zoning or aesthetics. Inevitably, Dallas looked like a town that sooner or later would have to pause for breath, be torn down, and then be built again with a rational eye for the needs of the future.

Old San Antonio was the state's hereditary showcase of its recent turbulent and often-violent past of Spanish missionary effort, revolution, Indian warfare, the forced blending of Mexican and Anglo-American cultures and a military tradition destined to last forever. Where Dallas choked itself, San Antonio sprawled, its streets wandering as aimlessly as the river around which the town had been growing fitfully since late in the eighteenth century. When the summer breezes blew from the south and the west, the city reeked vilely of stockyard aroma; the Mexican *barrio* was a quarter of poverty, filth, degradation and social crime. However, San Antonio was not without charm and turn-of-the-century trappings. An out-of-state newspaperman whose name has not survived the archival process commented that "where the unsightly Mexican cart once met the gaze you now see the beautiful and convenient street cars with their sleek, fat mules and their jingling bells." The anonymous recorder had been in San Antonio a generation previously and had been horrified by "ugly, filthy streets where a peaceable man and a decent lady dreaded to walk." Now he praised the attempts at paving, the flower gardens, the "sober, courteous policeman and on all sides the beautiful, well-dressed lady whose sweet smile of welcome makes one feel as if he had just met a morning zephyr passing through a grove of magnolias." San Antonio boasted of its new Opera and Civic House, and when Sarah Bernhardt's train paused at the Sunset Depot en route to New York from Mexico City, she impetuously declared to the crowd gathered at the foot of her private car, "San Antonio is the art center of Texas!" This was not strictly true—Galveston held the distinction —but to the citizenry anxious to brush aside the city's earthy past and enter some kind of cultural mainstream, Miss Bernhardt's words were rhapsodic.

Houston, fifty miles to Galveston's rear, was a brawling, hard-luck town sited between unpromising prairie to the north and swampy bayous everywhere else. The town was founded in 1836 by two brothers from New York, Augustus and John Allen, who lured immigrants from the East with extravagant newspaper ads. Westward-seeking pioneers came to Houston by wagon train, oxcart, on horseback and aboard flat-bottomed pirogues through fetid, mosquito-infested, root-tangled bayous only to find themselves in an oppressive climate where constant warfare was waged with mud, yellow fever and alligators. Many moved on, but others stayed, seeing promise that Houston could one day become a thriving port; after all, Buffalo Bayou led into the bay, thence into the Gulf of Mexico. Farmers looked past the swamps and saw vast acreage where crops could be grown. Painfully, Houston took root.

Promoters envisioned Houston as the state's future "great interior commercial emporium." Accordingly, the main street was run to the head of navigable Buffalo Bayou; but only shallow-draft paddle-wheelers and barges were able to take advantage of pickup and delivery of goods in the heart of town. Attempts to dredge a channel to the sea were a failure. Interior trade depended upon seven-teamed oxen struggling with heavy wagons up dirt roads turned into bogs by frequent downpours; merchandise was stranded, perishables were ruined and schedules were seldom kept. Freight rates climbed to the sky.

Railroads were needed, and railroads came; but only after a series of financial disasters brought on by far-visioned but short-funded promoters. Houston was visited by two conflagrations that gutted the business district only twelve months apart; recurring floods swamped the town, and casualties were high from whole series of epidemics, chiefly yellow fever carried by the millions of mosquitoes swarming in the bayous.

The city's greatest frustration, however, was the hard fact that deep-draft, seagoing ships could not approach the city directly. Galveston was getting the bulk of the ocean commerce that Houston somehow believed was rightfully hers. The much-heralded "Port of Houston" became a statewide joke, wounding civic pride. A visiting wit named Alexander E. Sweet infuriated the town's pioneers when he published his observations about the great port. Commented Sweet:

"The Houston seaport is of a very inconvenient size— not quite narrow enough to jump over, and a little too deep to wade through without taking off your shoes. When it rains the seaport rises up twenty or thirty feet and the people living on the beach, as it were, swear their immortal souls away on account of the harbor facilities. The Houston seaport was so low when I saw it last that there was some talk of selling the bridges to buy water to put in it."

When, shortly before the turn of the century, a Galveston merchant sent six bargeloads of salt to Houston via the bayou only to lose the entire shipment to a drenching rain that dissolved the lot onto the bayou's greenish waters, the urbane Galveston *News* did not lose the opportunity to jibe at Houston's pretensions. "Houston at last has a salt-water port," said the editor. "God Almighty furnished the water and [the merchant] Heidenheimer furnished the salt."

In 1900, Galveston could afford to be condescending toward Houston, whose struggles to become the great commercial emporium were obviously doomed to failure. Moreover, where Houston was unplanned and ugly, Galveston was neatly laid out with geometric precision. Great mansions marched in stately procession down Broadway, verdant with oleander, oak and palm trees. The city offered six public squares, two parks, crushed-shell paved streets, two miles of esplanade, three concert halls, an opera house, twenty hotels, and electric streetcars; the economy was fat with more than thirty stock companies backed by enormous capital. Public crime was rare in Galveston and people were unafraid of nighttime promenades to take advantage of the Gulf's cooling breezes. But no sensible person ventured on Houston's humid streets after dark; the town had a reputation for violence unmatched anywhere in Texas. Few days went by in Houston without some downtown saloon brawl ending in gunfire and death, incidents duly reported by the Galveston *News* on the front page.

Another reason for Galveston's pride—or, as Houston claimed, arrogance—was the fact that although Galveston's enviable status was achieved partially as a result of happy geological accident, most of its glory was due to the driving ambition of a select few hard-rock visionaries.

Galveston Island was no more than an elevated grassy sand bar twenty-eight miles long and from one to three miles wide when seen by the first Europeans. The island lay two miles off mainland America, providing shelter for an irregularly shaped bay cutting a thirty-mile-deep gouge into Texas. In 1528 a Spanish explorer named Alvar Nuñez— better remembered as Cabeza de Vaca—and a handful of followers were flung ashore with the wreckage of their small ship, battered by storms. They floundered through the salt marshes and the heavy grass, encountering an astonishing number of snakes and frightening herds of wild deer. Hostile Karankawa Indians swept upon the Spaniards, stripped them of arms and armor and kept them in hard captivity for six years. Nuñez and the survivors managed to escape, making their way back to Spain via Mexico City, where Nuñez wrote of his hardships. *Malhado,* he called the island, misfortune. But Spain was captivated by the idea that the long spit of sand was inhabited largely by snakes; it was put on the map as *Isla de las Culebras,* and was forgotten.

It wasn't until 1785 that the Spanish bothered to survey the island and the surrounding bay. They judged the waters too shallow for commerce, the island insignificant as a bastion. Nevertheless, they dignified the area with a name, Galvez, honoring Count Bernado de Galvez, Viceroy of Mexico. The surveyors sailed away, and the island remained in limbo for another thirty years. Then, in 1816, with a bloody revolution underway in Mexico to rid the country of Spanish rule, a Mexican flotilla of fifteen ships, outfitted as men-of-war, hove into Galvez Bay. The commander, Don Luis Aury, planted a Mexican flag in the dunes and announced his intention of blocking the passage of Spanish ships that had heretofore enjoyed a free hand in the Gulf. Galvez Island suited Aury fine, and a small settlement grew among the dunes, protected by captured Spanish guns pointing out to sea.

In the spring of the following year, Aury was joined by another adventurer, Francisco Xavier Mina, who brought another two hundred Mexican patriots to help share in what had become for Aury a lucrative business of plunder. After a while they asked themselves, why confine our efforts to the Gulf? Why not raid the Mexican coast itself? The expedition was readied by stripping the island of every able-bodied man and every gun. Within a week the ships were loaded and underway for the Mexican mainland.

Not two days out of Galvez Bay, Aury and Mina fell into a violent quarrel; they disagreed as to where to land and, more to the point, how the spoils should be divided. Finally, Mina sailed off in one direction, Aury the other. Aury milled around in the Gulf, indecisive, and finally settled on returning to Galvez, home and sanctuary. But when the island came into view he was astonished to see the harbor filled with ships. Mina's? He did not have that many. Brigs and sloops were deployed defensively and bristled with guns. When Aury discovered that the sinister armada belonged to the terror of the Gulf Coast, pirate Jean Lafitte, he prudently heeled his smaller craft around and sailed into historical oblivion.

Lafitte, thirty-seven, had been driven by the authorities from his Louisiana hunting grounds and knew a good thing in Galvez when he saw it: the bay offered snug harbor for his raiders; Spanish merchantmen could be easily plucked from the Gulf; and, most important, neither the United States nor Spain seemed to take the slightest interest in who controlled the Texas coast. Spain was embroiled in the Napoleonic wars at home, and the power of the United States was not yet equal to her desire for lands that far west of the Mississippi. With characteristic energy Lafitte began building a wildcat settlement which he named Campeachy.

On the eastern end of the island, facing the bay, Lafitte erected a sturdy two-story house within the confines of walls left behind by Mina and Aury. The walls were raised and strengthened with rock and sand, embrasures cut and wooden platforms built for cannon. The house was topped with a soaring observation platform where, with his strongest glass, Lafitte could observe the passage of ships far out in the Gulf. For good measure, Lafitte ordered a heavy cannon hoisted to the roof where it could be trained upon the periphery of his new empire. The first floor was sumptuously furnished with loot taken from ships of many nations; the rough-hewn tables were set with Belgian linen, English crystal, Spanish gold and silver. *Maison Rouge*, Lafitte called his island villa, and later visitors to the Red House were astonished at the pirate's cultivated tastes and expansive hospitality.

Around the walls of the new fort, rising above the grass, grew a ramshackle village. Lafitte knew where the money lay and he encouraged Campeachy in its efforts to become a pleasure island offering the basic satisfactions to the new Campeachians who flocked to the island by the hundreds:

pirates, highwaymen, open-air distillers, veteran prostitutes and eager learners, deserters from armies and navies of other nations, and Indian squaws who had learned how to profit from the white man's seamier ways. The settlement was given over to saloons, cribs, gambling dens, stills and, above all, slave marts kept under iron control by Lafitte himself, who set the price for black flesh at one dollar per pound. Importation of slaves into America had been illegal since 1808, but Lafitte found a ready market for this human cargo among Southern plantation owners.

For Lafitte's purposes, Galveston Island was ideal; his ships could easily slip out of the bay and into the Gulf for rich pickings that had only to be unloaded on the island for sale on the spot or, in the case of slaves brought in from the West Indies, put aboard shallow-draft boats and sent into Louisiana via the Sabine and other rivers feeding into the bay. Lafitte and his buccaneers waxed fat with profit and, unmolested as they were by any government, were prepared to stay at Campeachy until Spanish trade was drained of the last doubloon.

In January, 1818, several small boats filled with smartly uniformed soldiers beached on the island and the commander, forty-four-year-old General Charles François Antoine Lallemand, an ex-officer in Napoleon Bonaparte's *Grande Armée*, sought an audience with Lafitte. At dinner over silver goblets of Spanish wine, Lallemand outlined his ambitions to the pirate chieftain: he had brought his soldiers, two hundred men in all, all the way from Philadelphia in order to establish a French military colony in Texas. His dream, he said, was to help Joseph Bonaparte win the crown of Mexico—or at the very least to provide for the emperor safe refuge far from his enemies. Lafitte, who wanted no involvement with political affairs, would have nothing to do with Lallemand's mad scheme, but he did allow the Frenchman to set up camp some distance from *Maison Rouge* and watched in amusement as the dedicated dandies drilled, plotted and dreamed.

Two months later Lallemand and his troop crossed over to the mainland and built a pair of forts near an abandoned Spanish town called Atascosito. When word reached Lallemand shortly afterwards that the Spanish were marching in their direction, the band fled into Louisiana and disintegrated.

Meanwhile, in faraway Washington, D.C., President James Monroe had learned of Lallemand's presence in Texas, and the Frenchman's ambitions frightened him. Monroe, already thinking in hemispheric terms, wanted no armed French politicking in Texas, even though the territory still belonged to Spain. Monroe was watching with keen interest the progress of the Mexican rebellion and believed that the Mexicans would win their independence and, with it, Texas. He dispatched an emissary, Colonel George Graham, to Galvez to warn off Lallemand and, incidentally, to gather information about Lafitte, whose growing notoriety was making the President uncomfortable.

Graham reached Campeachy in August, 1818, only to discover that Lallemand had ceased to be a threat to future Mexican-American relations. Graham was impressed with the large-scale smuggling carried on by Lafitte—but he was far more captivated by the island's commercial potential. He wrote a lengthy report on Campeachy, pointing to the natural harbor and the proximity to the numerous Texas rivers that could become major interior inland waterways. "Galvez," he wrote, "is a position of much more importance than the

Government has hitherto supposed. It is the key to the greatest and best part of Texas." Graham concluded by urging that the United States take possession of the island without worrying further about Spanish attitudes or reaction. Spain's power was clearly dwindling, and the pirate Lafitte had expressed only the most amiable feelings toward the wishes of the American government. Graham's report, however, was pigeonholed in the office of the Secretary of State and forgotten.

By the end of two years' tenure of Campeachy the toll of Spanish ships sunk and captured by Lafitte rose to nearly a hundred, and not even the forces of nature could discourage him. In the fall of 1818 a hurricane invaded the Gulf and smashed at the island. Heavy winds carried away the flimsier structures, driving the bulk of the population inside the walls of *Maison Rouge*. The bottom floor of the big house admitted scores of women and children, but not even this bastion could withstand the fury of the storm. The top deck caved in and Lafitte's heavy cannon plunged down and crushed a dozen people. A flood tide swamped the island, ruining food stores and soaking caches of gunpowder. In the bay, sailors struggled to keep the ships afloat and many were flung into the turbulent waters and drowned. The hurricane passed, leaving Campeachy a shambles. Four of Lafitte's ships were sunk, others were dismasted and otherwise damaged.

To resurrect Campeachy meant staving off famine. Lafitte reduced the numbers to be fed by seizing a fast schooner that entered port from New Orleans and loading aboard every African-blooded man, woman and child whether free or not, and shipping them to Louisiana to be sold on the block. The population was further trimmed by the flight to the mainland of those Campeachians who pointed out that the next storm might be worse and that the island demonstrably offered no protection whatsoever against the terrible waters of the Gulf.

Lafitte reassembled Campeachy from the scraps of debris, and piracy and slaving went on as before. But the storm was only the beginning of Lafitte's troubles. One of Lafitte's captains, a recalcitrant man named Brown, violated standing orders by opening fire on a United States cutter. A lively cannon duel followed that ended with the cutter chasing Brown back to Campeachy. Furious, Lafitte ordered Brown hanged on the spot in full view of the American seamen. Brown was left swaying under the gibbet until, as one observer recalled, "his bones were picked by the birds on the sands of the bay."

Lafitte next had trouble with the Karankawas, who prowled the far western end of the island. The Campeachians and the Indians had lived apart, and therefore without friction, for almost three years. Lafitte had put the other end of the island off limits to his men, wanting as little trouble with the red men as he did with the American navy. One day, however, a hunting party from Campeachy ventured into the Indians' preserve and while bagging deer eagerly sought game of another kind. A young squaw was abducted and carried kicking back to the hunters' camp. Painted, howling Karankawas came after her and a pitched battle left four of the hunters dead and wounded with the others fleeing through the marsh grass for their lives. The Karankawas lived up to their reputation by cooking and eating all four of the pirates left behind.

Lafitte ordered a punitive expedition marched out of the

settlement to deal with the cannibals. The Karankawas met the pirates head on at a place called Three Trees, and for seventy-two hours the air was filled with the hiss of arrows, the crash of muskets and the cries of the wounded and the dying. Hard pressed, the pirates sent back for help. A pair of small brass cannon was taken from Campeachy's fortifications and dragged to the battlefield. Karankawa courage was no match for grapeshot, and the decimated ranks of Indians were forced to leave the field to their enemies.

Lafitte's island fiefdom was doomed shortly after the Battle of Three Trees. Another of his captains, apparently forgetting Brown, unsuccessfully attacked a second United States cutter and was brought back to Campeachy in chains. This time the hanging was done at the end of an American rope and Lafitte was ordered to clear out of Galvez for good. When Lafitte and his remaining followers sailed out of the bay Campeachy was left in flames. Only the charred remains of *Maison Rouge* were left standing as a reminder that men had ever lived there. Grass reclaimed the island, and only the cry of the gulls and the soft footfall of deer broke the eternal silence.

Galveston Island remained abandoned for another fifteen years while Mexico, Spain and Texas thrashed out their differences at such places as Mexico City, the Alamo and San Jacinto. With the defeat of the Mexican Army under Santa Anna, Texas declared itself an independent republic owing allegiance only to itself. The heady sense of freedom was dampened by the sober fact that the treasury of the new republic was virtually empty, and any avenue leading to commercial enterprise was eagerly explored.

In December, 1836, a one-time colonel in Sam Houston's

army, Michel Branamour Menard, excited the treasury's interest with an offer of $50,000 for "a league and a labor" of land on the eastern end of Galveston Island. The 4600 acres in question included the site of the ruins of Campeachy and the undeveloped harbor where Lafitte's ships had lain at anchor. Texas was glad to see the cash, and was even more interested in Menard's plans to develop Galveston as the greatest port city along the Gulf Coast, surpassing even New Orleans.

Menard was an energetic Frenchman who had migrated to Texas from Canada in the 1820s. His experience as a *voyageur* and trader in the Canadian wilds eventually led him to the post as Commissioner of Indian Affairs in Texas, a job that kept him on the move among the various tribes, where he proved to be not only an able but a sympathetic administrator. It was largely due to Menard's canny insight into the minds of the Great Plains Indians that he was able to block Mexican efforts to lure the Comanches and Apaches into an alliance with Santa Anna during the early stages of the Texan revolt. Part of Menard's reward for services rendered was election to the First Congress of Texas, but it was money Menard wanted, not power. As early as the fall of 1834 Menard had his eye on Galveston and had secured a land grant from Mexico's *empresario* in Texas, Juan Seguin. To Menard at the time, Galveston was "a wild project," but it seemed less so when the successful revolt obviated the problem of having to cope with the subtle labyrinths of Mexican law. Menard further had the encouragement and backing of a pair of shrewd businessmen, Samuel May Williams, whose wealthy brother in Baltimore was willing to pour money into the project, and Thomas F. McKinney, a man given to picking his teeth with a Bowie knife and to wearing frock coats made of scarlet blanketing trimmed in black.

Another seven backers were found, and a joint stock company was formed with one thousand shares valued at a thousand dollars each. Thus began the first serious effort to create a permanent settlement with long-range goals on the island. Boats were soon unloading polished mahogany boxes with surveying instruments inside, tools of the carpenter's trade, lumber, nails and general provisions for those who had come to Galveston from states as far away as Maine and Vermont. Wooden shacks sprang up on the island, and all day surveyors were at their transits peering through oculars offering dancing images of flat terrain warped by rising currents of warm air. The genial air of industry created a climate of enthusiasm, and Menard watched fresh capital begin to flow into the corporate coffers.

Then, in the fall of 1837, the gulf breezes changed into a cyclonic hammer roaring in from the sea. The newly planted trees were uprooted, the surveyor's shacks were swept away, and a wall of water erased the carefully placed pegs and lines that promised homes and stores for the future. The island was virtually stripped, but Menard's resolve was not; the work was done all over again and seven months later, on April 20, 1838, the Galveston City Company opened the sale of town lots to the public for 20 percent down, the rest to be paid later in annual installments.

There was no lack of prospects; immigrants were pouring into Texas, many of them lured into staying in Galveston by salesmen who met them at the boat. The streets were laid off with geometric precision, unlike any others in the entire state. The avenues ran east-to-west the length of the island, intersected by the streets running north-to-south.

Members of the corporation resisted the temptation to name these thoroughfares after themselves or after the numerous Texas heroes; instead the avenues were alphabetized, beginning with Avenue A near the bay, and the streets serialized, 1st Street beginning at the eastern end of the island. Thus orientation was no problem at all.*

Within a year Galveston could boast of a population exceeding 1000; there were 250 family dwellings of one kind or another, a post office, a customs house, two wharves and several warehouses, plus two hotels—one of them an abandoned steamboat dragged ashore and converted into a hostelry. Menard watched with satisfaction as an increasing number of ships entered the harbor to begin the foundations of coastal trade. With another hundred dwellings being thrown up slapdash on the island, Menard decided to erect his own showcase residence—located, to be sure, some distance away from the center of town. Far out on 33rd Street, Menard chose a large lot, but not even his burgeoning bank account could buy decent carpenters, which were in short supply not only in Texas but throughout the West. The solution was to buy a house prefabricated in the East and have it shipped to Galveston in one of the many nearly empty bottoms that arrived in Galveston to pick up baled cotton.

Late in 1838, Menard's house arrived from Maine. The siding, columns, capitals and studding were all premarked for assembly by local laborers. When completed, Menard's house stood two stories tall, a Greek Revival structure with wings on either side of the main building, the roofs supported by a total of eight wooden Doric columns. Trees

---

* But miscalculation and rigid adherence to the scheme resulted in drolleries such as "Avenue M½," "Avenue O½," and others. The avenues are so named to this day.

were planted and the house was christened, appropriately, "The Oaks." Menard's house was an exception, however; Galveston was growing rapidly, but, against the Corporation's hopes, not always handsomely.

In 1839, a young British diplomat was sent from Barbados to represent the Empire's interests in the Republic of Texas. Francis C. Sheridan, twenty-seven, an elegantly dressed Londoner and son of playwright Richard Brinsley Sheridan, arrived in Galveston aboard H.M.S. *Pilot* with his terrier, Nelly. He was not impressed. "The appearance of Galveston from the harbour is singularly dreary," he observed. "It is a low, flat sandy island . . . with hardly a shrub visible, and in short looks like a piece of prairie that has quarrelled with the mainland and disbanded partnership."

Sheridan observed that Galveston's terrain influenced men's fashions, commenting that "the costume most in vogue in Galveston is the blanket frock coat and trousers, with the simple and elegant alteration as to the general mode of wearing the trousers with the boots pulled over them. The nature of the soil on which Galveston is built, however, makes this eccentricity a comfort—it being a mixture of mud and sand generally up to the ankles of the pedestrian.

"This circumstance," continued Sheridan, "is productive of various complaints: yellow fever, ague, rheumatisms and others. When either a heavy rainfall or an irruption of the sea (a frequent occurrence during the prevalence of the 'Northers') the ground gets thoroughly soaked [and] the effect of the hot sun extracts such a horrible stench as no ordinary nose has smelt. In addition there is nothing fragrant in dead and decaying oysters which plentifully bestrew the streets to such an extent that, indeed, one of the principal medical men attributed much of the fever last summer to these Texian 'Powldoodies,' and suggested the suppression of the out-of-doors oyster trade during the sickly months of the year."

In Sheridan's ramblings around Galveston he was struck by the polyglot of tongues. "The population boasts members of every nation; English, American, German, Italian, Dutch and others. Of these, the Germans are infinitely superior as settlers, whether as agricultural laborers, tradesmen or mechanics. You never see a German idling, adding to which he is sober, peaceable and persevering. The rest of the foreign powers are not much distinguished for these qualities."

He noted that Galveston was sprinkled with Mexicans captured three years earlier at the battle of San Jacinto and who "preferred to earn their livelihood among their captors instead of returning to their own countrymen. In the simplicity of my heart," Sheridan admitted, "I should have believed them to be Chinese by their looks. They are utterly reckless of all things so long as their inordinate passion for cigars can be gratified, and they will willingly sacrifice their food to obtain them."

The wharf area fascinated Sheridan, who found it a showcase of contemporary America. "Here I once fell in with a settler who had just landed with a gang of slaves, one or two assistants, a driver, several long Kentuckee rifles and some large dogs. The only person in the party who appeared to be at all anxious about the result of the step he had taken was the proprietor himself. As for the Niggers, they laughed and chattered as if utterly careless of anything except enjoying themselves as much as possible. A cart was prepared for the transportation of the old women, the small children and the luggage—beds, cooking utensils and calabashes were all bundled into the cart, the young and the able each cheerfully shouldered some article for which there was no room.

"The driver coupled the dogs, having given each a preliminary beating to ensure respect on the road, and in a few minutes I was left alone gazing on the lessening train and listening to their laughter with melancholy forebodings."

On another day Sheridan joined a crowd peering down at a flat-bottomed barge. A corpse dressed in a faded blue uniform adorned with tarnished brass lay peacefully on the decking. In progress was a Galveston-style inquest into the death of the Navy Yard's chief clerk, knocked off the wharf in a drunken row the night before. "The crowd," noted Sheridan, "appeared to consider the loss of a man's life to be a matter of too common occurrance to permit either surprise or curiosity. Sitting 'round the gunwales of the boat, kicking their heels against the sides, sat the gentlemen of the jury, each smoking a cigar and enjoying himself as much as he could under the circumstances. [The inquest] lasted only three or four minutes, after which the jurors scrambled up the wharf, an old duster was thrown over the face of the deceased officer and he was left with none to honor him with even a glance."

Following death to its final conclusion, Sheridan visited the Galveston cemetery, east of town and bisected by a public road. "Far from romantically situated," he criticized, "or even judiciously, inasmuch as part of it merges with a swamp and some of the graves are filled with water. I remarked several large turkey buzzards in close consultation 'round a grave that had just fallen in. Besides this burying of one's relations in a swamp is not only productive of inconvenience, but in great measure mars the solemnity of living grief over

the loved dead. Conceive a widower mounted on stilts sobbing over the resting place of the lost partner of his affection, or a grateful son in shrimper's boots paying the last
tribute of filial affection to the authors of his being. Grief,"
Sheridan concluded, "ought to be dry."

Nothing pleased this Mayfair dandy, who complained of
the irregularity of the town "that straggled for about a half-
mile along the coast," and of the depressing series of frame
houses, too few of which had foundations of brick "brought
all the way from 'Bosting' for the moderate sum of 40 dollars
a thousand." He was shocked when a number of wealthier
residents confided that they "rather looked forward to the
probable destruction of this town by fire as an event to be
desired, because then those who could would then build
their houses entirely of brick."

And that is almost precisely what happened, but years
after Sheridan returned to England.

Even in its primitive stage of evolution Galveston continued to fascinate the foreign traveler, who saw in the fitfully growing town a distillate of American raw ambition,
hardheaded ability to recognize material potential, and ram-
bunctiousness—qualities long vanished in Europe and, especially to the British, somehow distasteful.

On a bright, brisk September morning in 1843 the
schooner *Dolphin* cleared out of Dover bound for America
via Madeira and the West Indies. Among the thirteen passengers aboard this luxuriously fitted 219-ton superyacht
were the E. M. Houstouns, an experienced man-and-wife
team of newspaper-feature writers commissioned by the London *News* to report on the face and the soul of the New
World. Of the two, Mrs. Houstoun proved the most astute

observer, the most prolific writer. At Madeira, she found a melancholy counterpoint to the island's bright sun and flowery hills in the "many wasted invalids, pale hectic girls and young men struggling against decay." At Port Royal, "as ugly a town as can be," her faithful Newfoundland, Wallace, fell in a fit while frolicking on the beach and died of sun-stroke. She was doubtful that the freedmen were better off than when servile to their Creole masters, for they "wandered about in rags and destitution; idleness is their occupation and drunkenness their striking vice." New Orleans was a welcome sight. "Such forests of masts! Such flaunting colours and flags, of every hue and every country! Really, as the Yankees say, Orleens may stump the universe for a city. Five tier of shipping in the harbour! The American breakfast is not to be surpassed in any other country; great variety of fish and fruit, preserves of every kind, and cakes of all sizes and descriptions. The buffalo tongues are praiseworthy, and so are the Philadelphia hams which they assert 'whip the Westphalia by a long chalk.' The buckwheat cakes, delicious when buttered and hot, but how unwholesome! Nothing but an American digestion could venture to indulge in them habitually."

On December 18, a cold day made unpleasant by fog and drizzle, the *Dolphin* shortened sail and prepared to enter Galveston harbor. The terrors of crossing the notorious sand bar guarding the approaches were well known, and the *Dolphin*, one hundred feet long, mounting six guns and drawing a full twelve feet of water, risked grounding unless she was guided in by a pilot. Crew, captain and passengers waited for uncomfortable hours, but the promised pathfinder failed to put in an appearance. Then out of the gloom appeared the steamship *New York*, puffing and blowing, looking to Mrs. Houstoun like "some huge elephant out of breath." The steamer's skipper cheerily offered to tow the yacht across the bar, thirty minutes' work, for the exorbitant amount of one hundred dollars. The offer was refused, but the *New York* shipped an experienced pilot aboard the *Dolphin,* and he explained what they must do to get the yacht into the harbor.

Unusually strong north winds had prevailed for days, blowing much water out of the bay, thus raising the bar to within inches of the depth of the *Dolphin's* draft; the vessel, he explained, would have to be "tripped" across. The guns were run forward and the ballast shifted, putting the yacht on dead even keel. The bow slipped forward slowly through the water, and after agonizing minutes the pilot announced they were across. Guns and ballast were reshifted and *Dolphin* eased through the tight confines of the channel, scraping the muddy sides as she went. The ticklish operations necessary to get the boat safely at anchor in four fathoms of water caused the Houstouns to wonder at Galveston's prospects as a major port city in the future.

A few days in Galveston convinced Mrs. Houstoun that "The Texans are an impatient people; they drive to, and at, their end with greater velocity than any individuals I ever saw or heard of. Nothing stops them in their go-ahead career. The present, and how to make the most of it, is their *idée fixe,* and they are too much occupied by their daily business to have leisure to think calmly of results." She watched in amazement as carpenters raised a six-roomed house, ready for habitation, in as many days. These clinker-built houses, it was admitted, were never meant to last more than ten years at the outside. They often lasted less.

On October 5, 1842, a year prior to the *Dolphin's* visit, a hurricane tore into Galveston and toppled half of the three hundred or so buildings that constituted the town. Many, built on wooden blocks to elevate the ground floor to keep out both floods and wandering hogs, were simply reraised and moved back into; few families, apparently, objected to living slightly canted. Houses reduced to scrap were replaced as quickly and as cheaply as possible. There were no casualties, other than damage done to the credibility of the local Roman Catholic priest. His church was the first to be blown on its beam ends, and the cleric sought refuge in the Protestant chapel to ride out the storm.

Like Sheridan before her, Mrs. Houstoun was often repelled by Galveston's more squalid aspects. In speaking of the town's muddy streets and the oozing patches of prairie that surrounded nearly every house, it seemed that the people "prefer enduring evils to losing time in remedying them. The pigs are the only ones who benefit, and they are as much considered and occupy as important a position in society as those in Ireland. These Galveston swine," she observed with disgust, "are not clean feeders, disputing carrion food with the turkey-buzzards. The pigs are frightful, their long tails destitute of curl, even when they retain the original number of joints. This, however is seldom the case. The dogs here are inveterate pig-hunters, and it is a rare sight to meet one of these unclean beasts with either ears *or* tail."

While riding horseback on the outskirts of the town's cemetery, she was shocked when her mount's forefoot casually kicked up a human skull. Looking around, she saw bones littering the soggy plain as though raked up by a giant hoe. "Trifles such as these," she commented, "are totally disregarded by these hardy settlers who make light of difficulties.

There is something very praiseworthy in this undaunted spirit of enterprise, and one feels that it deserves and will be rewarded by success."

And trifles they were; although Galveston was barely five years old, there was a rudimentary form of city planning in effect (but certainly no zoning laws); laid out on a draftsman's table were sketches of temples, public squares, theatres, botanical and zoological gardens and, above all, studies for docks and wharves for the seagoing commercial traffic that loomed in the future. There were four churches, schools, and no fewer than three newspapers to serve a community of some two thousand, not half of whom could be assumed to be literate.

Mrs. Houstoun wondered at the Galveston businessman's distaste at spending more than fifteen minutes at table to consume even the largest of meals; but he simply had not time, there were other things to do, and eating produced no income. Men went about the muddy streets with a purposeful air, amiable enough in greetings, gentle in manner, always ready with a quip—but their minds were elsewhere, their eyes gazing at some distant goal. Mrs. Houstoun astutely appreciated the reason for the Texans' behavior, the same reason why she believed Galveston would one day achieve its stated destiny of becoming the Queen of Port Cities, the New York of the Gulf of Mexico.

"The only apparent aristocracy in the United States," she wrote, "is that of wealth, and heaven knows the idol is in no want of worshippers. Those who in dress, appearance and so forth are decidedly the gentlemen of the land are so devoted to money-making that they neither have time, nor many ideas, to waste on other subjects. Their love of wealth being all-powerful, and being to be gratified only by

the strictest attention to business, it follows that the habits
of their lives generally become quiet and restrained . . .
[the people themselves] wearying and monotonous."

Galveston's founders would have been perplexed to learn
that the urbane Englishwoman believed their lives to be
either restrained or drearily repetitive. To men like Michel
Menard and Sam Williams, creating a city and nurturing it
into financial robustness was the most exciting career imagin-
able. The project had been given an added boost in 1845
by the United States annexation of Texas, a move welcomed
by almost every inhabitant who believed statehood would
bring a measure of financial and political security. Menard
watched the mercantile traffic increase month by month until
there were seven wharf companies sprawled along the bay
to handle the shipping. To Menard, this was six too many—
especially since a few of the wharf owners were not exploit-
ing this valuable space to the fullest but were merely holding
them as realty speculation. Together with Williams and
ten others, he formed a combine and took over the entire
port facility. Legally, the new organization was called The
Galveston Wharf & Cotton Compress Company and was
chartered as a semipublic concern. But in reality Menard
and his associates had created a true monopoly, charging
the limit in port and wharfage fees. That shipowners from
Liverpool to Baltimore called the company "The Octopus of
the Gulf" bothered the directors not at all; what was good
for the company was good for the city, and hence for the
state and the nation as well.

The entrepreneurial drive to put Galveston on a paying
basis was aided by a steady stream of immigrants pouring
onto the island from a Europe poor in opportunity and

torn by political and social upheaval. Slovak and Hungarian
Jews fleeing persecution and French farmers hoping to rid
themselves of wretched lives came in small scatterings. The
Germans, typically, were funneled into Galveston in organized loads, company and battalion strength. A 700-ton
ship, the *Iris,* was built in Bremen for the express purpose of
ferrying Germans across the Atlantic. The maiden voyage in
1856 successfully unloaded 240 passengers, all in sound
health and ready for work. Germans in Galveston, aligned
with moneyed uncles and cousins in the Old World, set up
profitable companies to handle immigration. Shipping mag-
nates in Bremen and Hamburg printed guidebooks for
American-bound Germans that pointed out the advantages
of selecting Galveston as a debarkation port; in this way
their ships could return to Germany loaded with cotton.
Richardson's *Texas Almanac* was translated into German
and more than 100,000 copies distributed on both sides of
the Rhine. By 1860, Galveston's population stood at slightly
more than 6500, 40 percent of whom were German by
birth.

The Teutonic influence was manifest in marked ways, not
the least of which was a refreshing attention to craftsman-
ship and an appreciation of the aesthetics of detail in the
building trades; new owners of German-built houses were
delighted to find that windows moved freely up and down
in their frames, even during sticky weather, and that the
hand-cut gingerbread moldings were beautifully finished,
fitting precisely between militarily upright Doric columns
neatly joined to porches that were plane parallel. Emigrant
German bakers, to whom corn was food for swine, weaned
the island away from that Southern staple, cornbread, by
introducing Rhenish loaves made from wheat milled on

machines of their own design. The Germans created reading rooms, social clubs, and a handsome casino with stage, proscenium and evocative scenery. *Kultur* extended to a beer garden and a bandstand; Sunday Galveston came alive with brass and drums, singing both nostalgic and Lutheran. With the islanders' acceptance of German folkways so skillfully blended into their own, the inevitable formation of a smartly uniformed rifle company created only enthusiasm. Armed with the most modern breechloaders available in Europe and gleaming with black patent leather and polished brass, the German Rifle Company was a colorful and exciting addition to Galveston streets on days of formal parade.

The arrival of the sober and aesthetically oriented Germans catalyzed the city administration's desire to recast the town's image. Money was appropriated to build a splendid new public park along Tremont Street, the main north-to-south thoroughfare, a park "similar to the ones we are told they have in Germany," explained the editor of the Galveston *Civilian*. Once the compulsion to spruce up the city took hold, there was no stopping it. Thousands of dollars were taken from the city treasury to provide the labor necessary to transport tons of clam shells to be crushed and packed down along a newly created bayside drive; "the better citizens of New Orleans" enjoyed evening carriage rides by the water, and so the Galveston gentry should also enjoy this same luxury. With this project complete, attention was turned to the ordinary streets, long the butt of jokes by visitors weary of ruining shoes and trouser and frock bottoms in cloying mud. At a cost of $740 per block, raised partially by a dollar-per-foot assessment of each householder, all of the business and main residential streets were shell-paved and kept dust-free in dry months by a water cart hauled by a mule. Sudden sunshine following rain turned the streets into broad avenues of mother-of-pearl, dazzling in their brightness.

Substantial business buildings began rising along The Strand. And at great cost. The three-story Hendley Building, four hundred feet long, was built almost exclusively of imported materials. The *Geranium,* out of Boston, off-loaded nine hundred tons of granite and five hundred barrels of Rosendale cement for this, the first "pretentious" business building, followed by three shiploads of the famous Boston brick—each one dipped by hand into hogsheads of water to properly cure the mortar. Four blocks away rose a new Customs House, a colonnaded, three-storied Greek Revival symbol of Federal authority. But it was in the homes that Galveston began to acquire architectural notoriety.

The moneyed mercantile class was growing in Galveston, and so were the number of homes; there were nearly a thousand dwellings on the island, but until 1859 not one of them was brick. James M. Brown, an uprooted Philadelphian who had made himself a millionaire by providing Galveston with hardware during the early building boom, decided to manifest his means by building a house unlike any other on the island. It would be all-brick, and it would be in the style of an Italian villa, a place where he and his wife could exhibit tastes cultivated in Europe while on tour. Brown had the interior walnut woodwork and gold-leaf mirrors carved in France. The rooms were so vast and the ornamented ceilings so high that massive furniture had to be built in order to preserve proportion. The somewhat forbidding exterior, deep red in color and austere of line, was relieved by uninhibited use of ornamental iron, worked in the shape of bunches of grapes and leaves mingled with sweeping whorls, romanesque arches and, here and there, subdued Grecian interlocking forms. The windows, a full story high on each of the three floors, were shuttered with white Venetian-type blinds. Surrounding the whole was a heavy cast-iron fence, shipped all the way from England, the gateposts whimsically topped with ripening iron ears of corn. Galvestonians were awed, and soon expensive architects were at work to create even more magnificent Xanadus.

Entertainment inside these coastal mansions was on a lavish scale. Some idea of how lavish can be gleaned by a report sent back to England by the British Consul, Arthur Lynn, who noted that in a typical year there were sold in Galveston twenty-three grand pianos, three thousand dollars worth of smaller musical instruments, 3665 gallons of good French wine and 786 gallons of imported brandy. Consul Lynn told the Earl of Clarendon that "the standard of living was dearer at this port than at any other in the United States." Lynn complained that the French and German consuls had long ago given up trying to reciprocate Galveston's social largesse and that even he, as Queen Victoria's representative, had to admit economic—and therefore, social—defeat.

The outbreak of the Civil War brought a quick stop to Galveston's spiraling development, but four years of varying occupation and blockade failed to maim the city's character or alter its hopes for the future. On March 2, 1861, the issue of secession was put to a referendum. The vote was nearly four to one in favor, with 14,697 Texans voting to stay in the Union.*

* Among those opposed to secession was Governor Sam Houston, then seventy. When he refused to take an oath of allegiance to the Confederacy he was promptly removed from office. He afterwards faced a hostile mob in front of Galveston's Tremont Hotel and thundered that secession would land the state "in fire and in rivers of blood."

A vastly superior Union navy threw a tight blockade around the island, cutting Galveston off from its world markets. Busy with the serious land battles raging in Virginia, the Confederates wrote off Galveston as being tactically impossible to defend. Consideration was given to putting the city to the torch and filling its wells with rubble and abandoning the island to the enemy. There were no supporters for this strategy among the islanders, but the big guns so laboriously placed for Galveston's defense were dragged away for use elsewhere and the city lay naked. After six months of blockade the Federals moved ashore and claimed Galveston for their own.

They kept it for eighty-eight days.

On the night of December 31, 1862, General John B. Magruder, CSA, invested the island from two sides, using four small ships riding low in the water due to an excess cargo of field guns, infantry and huge bales of cotton stacked on the decks as bulwarks against Union rifle fire and grape-shot. The Union garrison and the sailors on the ships riding at anchor in the harbor were not on the alert, a condition brought about by lack of action during the preceding weeks and, more acutely, by New Year's Eve excesses. The troops were landed and the guns manhandled ashore and put in position before dawn. At 5 A.M. the battle for Galveston opened with a sharp, and brief, contest for the city itself. The surprised and befuddled Federal troops were soon overwhelmed. Magruder's shore batteries and the guns aboard his "cotton-clads" began dueling with the Federal ships at first light. Spirited cannonading shook the cold morning air and the battle leaned back and forth until the Confederate ships closed and settled the issue with wild leaps by makeshift marines onto Union decks for hand-to-hand combat.

Wainwright, the Federal commodore, was killed aboard *Harriet Lane,* and the ironclad flagship *Westfield* was run aground and blown up to prevent capture; three other Federal ships stood out to sea and vanished over the horizon.

At a cost to themselves of twelve killed and seventy wounded, Galveston was once again in the hands of the Confederates, although it wasn't until too late in the war for the port's strategic value to be utilized. A large garrison was put ashore, but the islanders were quick to notice that no heavy guns were landed. The reason was obvious: big guns would require a great deal of time to transfer to the mainland, while troops could be gotten quickly to safety should the Federals think Galveston was worth retaking. Once again the blockade ships appeared in the Gulf, leaving the city to face an enemy on one side and indifference on the other. Galveston was expendable.

Left to its own devices, the city survived first by servicing the needs of the garrison. As quickly as Confederate dollars appeared in the form of government payrolls they as quickly were taken into Galveston's mercantile tills. One by one the southern ports fell: Charleston, Wilmington, Mobile. As the war dragged to a close Galveston came alive once more as a seafaring town of importance, an island base for daring blockade-runners sliding across the sea to Europe and the West Indies to barter cotton for arms and drugs. When Lee offered his sword to Grant at Appomattox, hundreds of bales of cotton lay on Galveston's wharves, ready for world markets. Business leaders who had been treading water on the island during four years of virtual limbo saw in these undelivered bales—soon confiscated by the bluecoats—not spoils of defeat but solid promise of the Queen City's manifest destiny.

Alone of the strategic Confederate cities to escape physical
or financial ruin, Galveston was a magnet for postwar seek-
ers of personal fortune. Morris Lasker had fled from Prussia
at the age of sixteen, crossing the Atlantic aboard a clipper
ship to land in Portsmouth, Virginia. Lasker, a classical
scholar who knew Hebrew and Greek but no English, saved
enough money working as a clerk to buy a one-eyed horse
and a wagon loaded with utensils with which to work his
way to Texas as a peddler. The trip took Lasker three years.
When war came he joined the army and took part in the
seizure of Galveston from the Federals. The island en-
tranced him, and with what little money he could scrape
together peddling to ranchers he came back to Galveston
and entered the wholesale grocery business. Acumen coupled with booming opportunity led him into real estate, flour
milling and banking. Within fifteen years Lasker was living
in a French Renaissance palace on Broadway and was
wearing a black silk hat on Sundays, the recognized symbol
of a man who earned $5000 a year or more. In Lasker's
case it was much more. He became in fact a millionaire
philanthropist whose voice was often sought in questions of
civic progress. Lasker never ceased to marvel at reaching
this heady plateau; Jewish peddlers who remained in Prussia could have no such ambitions.

William Lewis Moody arrived in Galveston at the advanced age of thirty-eight by a circuitous route that began
in Chesterfield County, Virginia. Moody, one of thirteen
children, was orphaned at the age of fifteen, but made it
through law school on his own and headed West. In Pitts-
burgh he decided to go to New Orleans by river steamer,
and from there he laid a course for Dallas. With the last of

his money he bought a tired-looking horse in Houston and started riding north. He got as far as Fairfield, Texas, when his mount simply lay down and died. "Moody," a new acquaintance said, "you stay here in Fairfield. This is the capitol of Freestone County, boy!" With little more than a change of shirts and the law diploma in his saddle bags, Moody had little choice. An illiterate hotel owner backed the tall Virginian in a law practice, but most of the clients were penniless and fees were paid out of the skimpy county treasury. The shingle came down and Moody opened a mercantile venture that provided enough steady income to get married on and start with the first of six children.

When the war came Moody raised G Company, Seventh Texas Infantry, and marched them to Kentucky. Almost the entire regiment was taken prisoner with the fall of Fort Donelson, but an exchange allowed Moody to take the field again in time for the battle at Jackson, Mississippi, on July 10, 1863. He was carried away so badly wounded the brigadier wrote him a commendation and sent him back to Austin for garrison duty until the end of the war.

The war had pointed up the overriding importance of cotton and wool to Everyman; Europe was starved for fibers and the final year of fighting had seen Confederate troops wearing captured Yankee uniforms turned inside out or splotchily dyed in chicory coffee. Cotton was again king, but Fairfield, Texas—250 miles from the sea—was no place to create a throne. Moody sold his mercantile business and moved to Galveston. He opened a commission office in the Hendley Building, still scarred by Magruder's cannonballs, and from his office could gaze on the satisfying vista of a forest of masts filling the harbor, the ships waiting for their baled loads.

The volume of cotton moving out of Galveston swelled, and so did profits. Moody opened a branch office in New York and a few years later was able to move out of rented quarters and into a building of his own in the heart of the Strand, four stories tall and built with bricks made in his own yards. Moody was asked by Governor Richard Coke to go to Wall Street and sell $2 million in state bonds to help bail Texas out of financial difficulties brought on by the recently deposed Reconstruction government. Moody, a self-made capitalist and no professional politician, talked bankers' language and succeeded far beyond Coke's expectations. When Moody's son and namesake reached his majority and entered the cotton factorage, he came with a prep-school and V.M.I. education coupled with travels in Europe. He agreed with his commodity-oriented father that there was money to be had in handling goods, but insisted that money itself was a commodity like any other, always in demand, incapable of reaching surplus, and not affected by vagaries of weather or subject to blight. The W. L. Moody & Company private bank was created, later absorbing the National Bank of Texas to become one of the largest private institutions of its kind in the state.

Much of the rapidly accumulating capital in Galveston was poured back into the city in the form of loans for developing new business ventures, improvement and expansion of already booming commercial concerns, and outright gifts for schools, parks, playgrounds, churches and libraries. The city invested in itself, and prospered accordingly. For anybody who wanted to work, there was a job; thus, of the evils visited upon mankind, poverty was the easiest to avoid in Galveston. Economic progress was further advanced by remarkable civic harmony, considering the polyglot of races, nationalities and attitudes making up a community living in the island's close confinement. Along the busy wharves, Galveston's thriving money pump, relations were serene between the predominately black workers and white management; goods flowed smartly in and out in a steady stream broken only once by strike or stoppage.

That black men predominated among longshoremen before the turn of the century was not because stevedoring was considered demeaning by whites—wages, in fact, were comparatively high—but was due to a bold exercise in economic racial equality long before the phrase "civil rights" entered the workaday national lexicon. In 1883 Galveston's white longshoremen walked out en masse and stayed out. The port verged on total shutdown. Faced with the loss of millions in revenues Galveston businessmen sought out Norris Wright Cuney, generally accepted as the spiritual leader of Texas Negroes. Would Cuney supply the workers needed to get the port back into full operation? Yes, Cuney replied, he would be glad to do so provided blacks were paid the same as whites. Wharf directors granted this extraordinary concession, Cuney organized the Negro Longshoremen's Association, the port reopened with no friction, and Galveston resumed its preeminence along the coast.*

Favored though it was, Galveston was still categorized by the U.S. Government as a third-class harbor—that is, a har-

---

* A stevedore's day was ten hours long in a six-day week. Wages were just under a dollar a day, but trained secretaries in large cities earned only ten dollars per week. At the time, however, sugar was four cents per pound, eggs fourteen cents per dozen, corn thirty-three cents a bushel, gingham was five cents a yard. A new Stein-Block suit could be had for ten dollars on sale, breakfast in a rooming house was seldom more than fifteen cents, and bourbon whiskey was going for two dollars a gallon.

bor that would not admit ships drawing more than twenty feet of water at mean high tide. And even as a harbor of the third class, the outer bar limiting the draft to twelve and a half feet put Galveston far down the scale.

The Federal Government was concerned because in the 750-mile stretch between New Orleans and the mouth of the Rio Grande at Port Isabel at the bottom of Texas there was not a single harbor of Class I or Class II. As early as 1884 an extensive survey was completed in which Washington concluded that "Galveston was the most suitable harbor on the Texas gulf coast for development." One reason was the fact that many big railroads and branch lines terminated there, another was the fact that $30 million worth of merchandise was exported from Galveston during a fiscal year in which only $1 million cleared out of all the other Texas ports combined. In faraway Denver (1150 miles from Galveston), support for deep water came from Governor John Evans, who realized that Colorado's development hinged on being able to get territorial goods to world market cheaper and faster than by hauling them by rail all the way to New York and other eastern ports. What Evans wanted was a deep-water port for Denver, and Galveston seemed the logical choice. In Galveston itself, William Lewis Moody chaired the Deep Water Commission, and pressure came from all sides to make of the city a Class I harbor. The only opposition came from the operators of the lighters that trundled goods back and forth across the sandbar to waiting ships, a service that made the owners rich but would become useless once deep water was achieved. The smaller ports of Sabine Pass and Aransas Pass opposed financial aid to Galveston for deep water, and serious infighting flared up when it came time for Congress to vote on appropriations in a river and harbor bill. Opposition to funding money to Galveston was answered by Congressman William D. Kelley of Pennsylvania.

"Whoever will look at a map of our country," he said, will see that Galveston is the port of entry for the vast region that is almost inaccessible to foreign commerce by the Atlantic ports. The people of Denver have a chance for the advantages of ocean trade from the nearness of the harbor of Galveston.

"We look at the long lines of roads which are to carry Denver's productions or their importations and we see that thousands of miles of land carriage intervene. But when we look at the Gulf seaports and our eye rests on Galveston, we see that [only] a thousand miles brings Denver and Pueblo to deep-sea soundings, and to a port in which already a large foreign commerce has concentrated. I am," warned Kelley, "prepared to protest against any action which shall delay the deepening and improvement of Galveston harbor for all that Rocky Mountain region." Kelley then added that a new railroad, the Denver & New Orleans, was already being built by John Evans to link up Denver with the sea.

A limp Congress appropriated a million dollars for the job, about one-sixth the amount of money actually needed to make Galveston a Class I harbor, and another four years of wrangling, debate and invective followed before the Board of Engineers' report that Galveston was the only harbor in Texas feasible for full development was accepted. The owners of the profitable lighter fleet at Galveston and the mayors of Sabine Pass and Aransas Pass, north and south of Galveston respectively, sulked their way into 1889 when work on the deep harbor project actually began.

To create deep water where no deep water exists means

gouging a vast trench in the alluvial bottom of the sea; this can be most efficiently done by harnessing nature to work against itself. Two long granite arms were sunk in the water leading from the bay to the open sea, built of 1½ million tons of granite quarried from the hills of central Texas. The arms, three miles apart at the base, narrowed to a mile and a half in open water: the south jetty was six miles long, the north, five. Before the jetties were built, ebb tide waters flowed out of the bay through a wide waste, dissipating the force and depositing suspended sediment as they eddied into the still waters and feathered into the littoral currents of the Gulf. Now, however, the outgoing tide was forced through the narrow outlet formed by the long granite arms, and the resultant increase in velocity not only forced the sediment outwards but scoured the floor of the Gulf, blasting through the sand bar, in a perpetual scooping action. When completed at a cost of nearly $7 million and five years in time, the jetties gave Galveston a free channel more than 400 feet wide with a depth of 26½ feet. Visible proof of Galveston's new status as a Class I harbor was given when the hulking battleship *Texas* plowed easily up the new channel to appear in the bay off the Strand. Cheers shook the town.

The new channel immediately added to Galveston's luster and riches; within the first year nearly two million tons of additional shipping cleared the harbor, and continuing bumper cotton crops assured the city of a shining future. By 1900, Galveston was indeed the Queen City. Recalled a young Texan named John W. Thomason, Jr., there for a summer visit with his grandfather: *

* Thomason later had a distinguished career as an officer of the United States Marines, authored and illustrated several books.

"It is remembered that the year 1900 opened auspiciously for the city of Galveston, pleasant in the sunlight, on the thin island athwart the bay where the Trinity River empties into the Gulf of Mexico; and that it continued so throughout the summer. Certain controversial matters vexed the place not at all: it watched idly the debate as with which century, Nineteenth or Twentieth, the year 1900 should align: the Vatican said with the Nineteenth, until January 1, 1901; and the famed Galveston *News*, Nestor of Southwestern family journals, sided with the Pope in Rome and lost no circulation thereby. Otherwise, the first halftone photographic reproduction in its history appeared in the *News*—a portrait of General Conje, lately captured by the British in the South African War. Queen Victoria was drawing to the end of her immense reign and received favorable comment in the American press: the blameless McKinley was coming up for his second term: there was trouble in the Philippines and a far-off brawl in China: the Republic was turning imperialistic, and editorial opinion held widely for expansion and manifest destiny. Galveston itself pointed with pride to the Federal census which gave it a poulation of 37,789 souls.

"Those days it was the custom of gentlefolk from the up-country towns to summer at Galveston. The Gulf breeze cooled the city at nightfall; one of the most beautiful beaches in the world offered delightful surf-bathing; and you saw everybody there in the afternoons, bathing, promenading or driving in carriages on the smooth, crisp sands. There were ample hotels providing luxurious accomodations for the wealthy, and a score of lesser hostelries invited the more prudent spenders. Bettison's Pier on the north jetty was an unrivalled fishing establishement: Murdock's Restaurant over the surf a splendid place to eat and to watch the waves. As to the city, it was lovely: its flat white buildings stood up from the water with the thin aspect of unreality; its streets were lined with oleanders; its lawns shaded by numerous palm trees; its verandas deep and draped with vines.

"We spent that summer in a little comfortable house about 21st Street north of Broadway. I remember the big surf that piled in, on a steady southeast wind, through the last half of August so that we had strict injunction against venturing beyond the first ropes on the beach. And all that month the tides ranged high on the wharves; the southeast wind drove in the tides and held them. The bay was brimming full by the end of August. I remember also rains that swamped the rudimentary drainage system and sent water two feet deep along Broadway, wherein we waded joyfully in bathing suits, rain and water and air alike tropic-warm.

"We departed upstate, on schedule, the first of September, I very reluctant, looking back to the low white city from the mile-long wooden trestles of the railroad bridge. That city as it was I never saw again, nor some of the boys and girls I knew there. . . ."

What young Thomason could see from a child's-eye perspective in looking up Broadway was a luxuriantly cultivated jungle of fig, orange and oleander trees rising above clusters of evergreen shrubbery and black Hamburg grape vines partially obscuring an awesome fairyland of palace- and castle-like homes looming against the sky. Broadway, 150 feet wide, with a 36-foot manicured esplanade down the middle, was the Gulf Coast's showcase of solid wealth and turn-of-the-century architectural grandeur. James Brown's Italianate villa, which had created such an impression when completed in 1858, had been eclipsed in size and sheer opulence again and again in a great residential building extravaganza that reached its peak in the late 1880s. Overwhelming was the massive home built by Colonel Walter Gresham, attorney and railroad tycoon, for his wife Josephine. Great circular and hexagonal towers, four stories high, bulged from an ornately heavy granite and red limestone façade. The towers, inset with myriad windows, were capped with both Medieval and Renaissance tiled cones. Slender circular chimneys, both functional and false, grew out of various levels of the upper reaches of the building like ancient stalagmites. The total effect resembled a museum of natural history, or a kind of château designed by a series of castle builders from various centuries. The bulking structure stood on but a single plot of ground, allowing no great sweep of landscape leading to the blue granite steps at the entrance, but Gresham considered that his $300,000 was well spent; the palace stupefied everybody who saw it.

By 1900 the once ramshackle area at the eastern end of town, not fifteen minutes' walk from Gresham's great oaken doors, was transformed into an acceptable middle-class neighbor and counterpoint to Broadway's stateliness—but a major disaster had been required to bring about the change. The great conflagration wished for in Sheridan's day waited until the morning of November 13, 1885, when the Vulcan Iron Works blazed up in a shower of industrial sparks and molten metal. The plant, located on the bay, stood next to an area where wooden houses were packed next to each other in flammable ranks. Had there been no wind, or a wind out of the south, the chances for confining the fire to the Works alone would have been good, for Galveston was justly proud of its smartly uniformed firemen. But an unusual thirty-knot wind blew in from the north at about the time the flames roared up and the fire was driven almost horizontally from one house to another, leaping across Broadway in a swath two to four blocks wide until it reached the waters of the Gulf on the other side of the island. Forty blocks were consumed and more than four hundred houses were burnt to ashes.

When the $2 million rubble was cleared away a phoenix of new houses eventually rose to reclaim the wasted acres. For the most part they were painted gleaming white and were handsome, but the new foundations were little better than the old; pick and shovel had to bite only four feet into the ground in that part of town before striking water.

# Chapter 3

## WEATHERMAN

ON FRIDAY MORNING, September 7, 1900, the storm-warning flags were run up over Galveston and snapped smartly in the breeze. Minutes later the telephone in the Weather Bureau office on the fifth floor of the Strand started ringing. The insistent jangle would continue until the next evening, until the lines went dead.

To the ordinary citizen, the sudden appearance of the unwelcome flags came as a total surprise. True, the waves had been unusually rough for the week past, but this only added exhilaration to the sport of riding the breakers and was an added bonus to the zestful crowds that packed the beaches on Labor Day when the temperature stood in the nineties. Ship masters just in during the last forty-eight hours had passed the word along the wharves and at home about how choppy and windy were the waters between New Orleans and Galveston, and deckhand and fireroom gangs spending the afternoon inside the white-fronted bordello on Post Office Street held forth on the dangers in the Gulf at that time of year; but Galveston was used to talk of storms, and having been victimized by the elements in varying degrees over the years, the people were not easily intimidated.

Nor had warnings reached them through the efficient Galveston *News,* although the paper ranged widely and well in its coverage of the world. From Monday through Thursday the front page was given over to news of how three had died in a Chicago heat wave; a large headline about the gathering of the Boxers in faraway Tientsin; a photograph of King Oscar, monarch of Sweden and Norway; a story of a minor riot along New York's West 48th Street caused by an apple core flung by a black boy at a white pushcart vendor; news of William Jennings Bryan's campaign in the east; and, more locally, brief items about rain in central Texas and news that the cotton crop would be coming late that year. Not until the storm flags were already up over Galveston was notice taken in the *News* on Friday that a great storm was raging in the Gulf; but the reader had to search diligently to find it: nine lines at the very bottom of the page, just above an illustrated ad for Royal Baking Powder.

Datelined Jacksonville, the brief item described high winds and downing of telegraph wires; the storm was "said to be northwest of Key West, Florida." But of course this news was trailing far behind events; at the time it was published the eye of the hurricane was near New Orleans, and moving fast.

From an open window in the Levy Building, Dr. Isaac Monroe Cline peered at the bowl of sky shimmering above the Gulf of Mexico. The usual signs heralding the approach of a hurricane were lacking; Cline noted that "the brick-dust sky was not in evidence in the slightest degree." Overhead only wispy shreds of cirrus marred the purity of pale blue, moved along by winds at altitude out of the southwest. Cline, a month shy of his thirty-ninth birthday, had been with the U.S. Weather Service nearly twenty years, the last eleven of them as Section Director and Chief of the Galveston Bureau, and as a veteran meteorologist he was not fooled by the pleasing skies. Cline had been tracking the storm through advisories sent out from Washington, D.C., for the past seventy-two hours, and when he ordered the square storm-warning flags sent up that morning he was ready for the incoming calls.

He could not say, of course, that Galveston would be the primary target of the large hurricane then boiling its way through the Gulf, but caution and a sense of potential disaster is a necessary ingredient of any good weatherman's makeup—and Cline's had been bought with long experience and an intelligence keener than most.

Cline, born on October 13, 1861, was a Tennessee farmer's son, and grew up with soil under his fingernails and an intense environmental curiosity; he spent hours away from his chores observing the crows winging over the fields of grain, field mice scampering through the corn, spiders spinning webs under rafters in the barn, and the dumb patience of his father's livestock in fair weather and foul. Above all, he was fascinated with the effects of the seasons' cyclic changes and the occasional violent outbursts from nature upon the land and those who lived on it.

Isaac Cline left the farm when he was sixteen and entered Hiwassee College, where he earned enviable marks not only in the sciences but in Greek and Latin. He graduated four years later, having long since decided to make a career out of the weather. The U.S. Weather Service was then a function of the Signal Corps, whose officers were happy to train the small, dapper and energetic Cline as a meteorologist at Corps Headquarters at Fort Meyer, Virginia. He was sent to Little Rock, Arkansas, on his first assignment and handled the routine duties with such ease that he found time to make an exhaustive study of the effects of climate upon the habits and movements of the common locust. This in turn led Cline into advanced biology, and from there Cline plunged naturally into medicine: he enrolled in the University of Arkansas and his quick mind and hard hours of work enabled him to win a degree as an M.D. in only three years. When, in 1885, Cline was sent to Abilene, Texas, to open a First Order Weather Station he was probably the most overqualified observer in the state.

Cline's distaste for idleness, coupled with the desire to add to his meager government salary, led him to yet another career field. At age twenty-five, and with no previous journalistic experience, he took over as editor and publisher of the faltering Abilene *Daily & Weekly Reporter* and soon had the paper running in the black. With what little leftover time he had, Cline sought out Abilene's diversions, but they were few indeed. He spent most Sundays in church because he was fond of music, and these frequentings resulted in marriage to the church organist, Cora Mae Bellew, on December 10, 1887. In the Cline tradition, no time was lost, and his first daughter was born nine months later.

In March, 1889, the chief of the U.S. Weather Service, tough old General Adolphus Greely, ordered Cline to Galveston to organize the Texas Section of the Service. Cline bought a large two-story white frame house at the corner of 25th Street and Avenue Q, only three blocks from the rolling surf. Characteristically, once the weather Section was well organized he joined the prestigious Galveston Medical School and pioneered as an instructor in medical climatology. Not long after moving to Galveston the Clines were blessed with their second child, another girl.

But the new Chief of the Texas Section was not as blessed in his choice of an assistant, a West Point graduate who had been cashiered because of addiction to whiskey brought on by the tedium of peacetime garrison duty. But he assured Cline that he had successfully undergone the rigors of the famous "Keely Cure" and was now as sober as a Baptist. Months passed, and the Keely alumnus showed no signs of weakening. But the routine, and not overly taxing, job of reading barographs, checking wind gauges, rain gauges and thermometers at precise intervals and noting everything in the log proved to be as monotonous as army life. Cline returned from lunch one afternoon to find the weather office cluttered with bird cages, the room alive with the trills and cheeps of a dozen species. The West Pointer was sitting on the floor in alcoholic euphoria. Cline sent him home to sleep it off, struggled downtown with the cages and returned them to the dealers and fired the bird fancier the following morning.*

---

* The Weather Service attracted its share of bon vivants. One New England observer filled his office with sophisticated camera equipment used, it was

On July 1, 1891, the Weather Service was shifted from its awkward status as a branch of the Signal Corps and transferred to the Department of Agriculture, a logical move at the time because America's large number of farmers had more interest in the weather than did any other group. Professor Mark W. Harrington, editor of a meteorological journal, replaced Greely; with a change in administration he was himself replaced by another political appointee, Professor Willis L. Moore. Not long after the outbreak of the Spanish-American War in 1898, Moore summoned Cline to Washington, D.C.

The new Weather Chief told Cline that he had just concluded a meaningful conference with the President, and McKinley stated, "Moore, I am more afraid of a West Indian hurricane than I am of the entire Spanish Navy." Moore told McKinley that he had every reason to be; figures at hand showed that more United States naval vessels were sunk by weather than by enemy action. Well, McKinley said, the admirals want better forecasting of weather conditions in the operational area, and what did Moore suggest? Moore directed the President to a large wall map and laid a finger on the province of Yucatán, the thumblike peninsula jutting into the Gulf of Mexico and pointing like a gun at Cuba, only 150 miles eastward. Moore explained that observation stations set up there and elsewhere along Mex-

---

discovered, for photographing society belles in the nude. A weatherman in the Midwest was fired on the spot when a government inspector caught him making observations in the town's hockshop; the instruments were in pawn to cover heavy gambling losses. Cline was required to investigate a colleague "who kept a fancy apartment where he bathed women in Florida water." The husband of one such bathee arrived unexpectedly and the weatherman locked the wife in a wardrobe and fled out of the window under pistol fire. General Greely fired more than one hundred observers during his first year in office.

ico's coast would be of the utmost advantage in helping American ships steer clear of developing weather.

That Cline was chosen by Moore to journey to Mexico City to complete negotiations with the autocratic government of President Porfirio Díaz is an indication of his standing in Washington. Moore had picked the right man; not long after Cline reached the National Palace the first U.S. weather observation station was set up and running in Tampico, followed by others in the towns of Progreso and Mérida in Yucatán. Cline had shrewdly capitalized upon the Mexicans' still-smouldering hatred of the Spaniards, the *gauchapins*, against whom weather information could conceivably be used. Moreover, he explained, the data would be useful to Mexican fishermen plying Gulf waters.

His entry into the jungles of Yucatán coincided with a rampaging yellow fever epidemic. Cline, M.D., earned the admiration of *campesinos* and authorities alike through long hours spent treating fever-stricken Indians, saving some and losing others. Like Walter Reed, Cline was convinced that mosquitoes were carriers of the dreaded yellow jack, and by carefully screening his rooms where he slept he managed to avoid the disease.

Dewey's defeat of the main Spanish battle fleet at Manila in May left only a squadron of the enemy ships blockaded at Santiago de Cuba. On July 3, 1898, the Spanish commander sortied from the harbor and on a clear, fine day his ships were destroyed one by one by the waiting Americans. Two weeks later the town itself fell to ground forces, and Cline's Mexican job was at an end. He returned to Galveston with the conviction that "The commander who knows his weather will win the battle, when another who does not will lose."

Cline's apprehension about the fate of Galveston on that weekend in September, 1900, was caused not only by the bulletins that reached him describing the approaching storm's magnitude, but by the island's past weather history and the city's almost total defenselessness against incursions by the sea.

Cline's records showed that since 1776, when a storm rushed ashore near Galveston to destroy an early Spanish mission, the Texas Gulf Coast had been struck by no fewer than forty-six tropical cyclones of widely varying intensities. Of these, a dozen had wheeled inland at or near enough to Galveston to cause damage ranging from broken tree limbs to inundation of the entire island. Storms had loomed out of the Gulf as early as the beginning of June and as late as the beginning of November, but the worst had occurred on October 3, 1867, just as the city was climbing into post-war prosperity. Cline could read first-hand reports of this storm, anticipating what might happen to Galveston within the next twenty-four hours. Wrote one eyewitness:

"All Wednesday night the strong winds from the east prevailed, increasing early Thursday morning accompanied by rain. The water began to rise and overflow the island, creeping up from one street to another until, at noon, it reached as high as Church Street. The lower floors of the stores on the Strand were from two to four feet under water and goods and property damaged to the amount of nearly a quarter of a million dollars.

"The wharves were submerged by the waves, and vessels tied up there were chafed and damaged. Lumber was floating through the streets and signs were more plentiful on the waters than on the houses. Hacks and drays were covered with passengers, hunting high ground. Merchants were hunting laborers to remove their goods from lower floors to higher places, and paying them as high as $6 an hour to do so. Vast piles of salt along the sidewalks of the Strand melted away and returned to mother sea, leaving the sacks where they belonged. Sugar boxes in the warehouses gave out their sweetness to the deluge. The great top-knot of the front of Sauter's building came down with a crash that startled the whole town. The third story of the new brick hotel was blown down on the Odd Fellows Hall, crushing it to a shapeless mass of splintered boards, and later in the day the next lower story came down.

"Most of the slate roof of the Masonic Hall was torn off. Freedman's Hall was blown down, and one man killed. The water submerged Mechanicsville, doing great damage to property in that vicinity, which is on very low ground and covered with water in even ordinary high tides. The bayous were all out of bank, spreading water in places entirely across the island. The city railroad track was submerged and the trains stopped running at an early hour. Sheds and galleries and china trees were twisted off by the wind, and fences blown down in every part of town. A drenching rain accompanied the storm all day; the yellow fever patients, the doctors say, will feel the change in the air in spite of every precaution and advise us to look for increased mortality in consequence.

"The water on the Gulf beach was belly-deep to a horse. The railroad depot was so battered by the rough waters of the Gulf that the blocks on one side gave way and the building settled to the ground. The wind was much more violent on the Gulf shore than in the city, and a good many buildings erected by the U.S. Army were blown down. The cemetery was covered with water a foot deep, and the ground to westward as far as the eye could see was a sea of water. Ships were damaged or sunk and the wharves presented the most completely wrecked appearance we have ever witnessed. The water at midday had so completely inundated the gas works that it was impossible to build fires, and the city was without light."

Also at hand for Cline's perusal was a report written by a veteran meteorologist, Professor C. G. Forshey, who watched the onset of the storm from inside his frame house. Recounted the professor:

"Before dawn the windstorm was upon us, blowing with vigorous blasts from the east, the sea beating with tremendous force upon the eastern end of the island. At 7 A.M., wind 15 degrees N. of east. This direction is slightly oblique to the coast line and will drive water into the bay. Temperature, 80 degrees. The whole heavens are portentous, and the fury of the gale increases as the rain sets in.

"8 A.M.—Wind, rain and temperature unchanged. Trees and fences giving way and slender buildings falling.

"9 A.M.—Drifting rain renders objects invisible at a distance. Think we can see ship masts (at times) out of their place. Wind increases, and water stands without draining off.

"10 A.M.—No abatement of violence. The wind has prodigious force. The sea appears nearly all over town. Looking west and north—cannot see far. (What a morning for funerals!)

"My neighbor, a young maiden, the mirth of her family, has expired in the full fury of the storm. To bury her now is impossible, except in a sea of water. The pestilence cannot pause for the tempest! (Have they combined for the utter desolation of our fair city?)

"There is no human form on these streets. Thermometer stands at 81 degrees. Wind—full N. of east."

Two hours later Forshey learned of the destruction of several of the larger downtown buildings, and at 1 P.M. he scribbled in his log that "a man can scarce keep his feet in the wind." With professional detachment, he determined to measure the velocity of the howling gusts, but in an unorthodox and ingenious way.

"Have no watch. Clock ticks twice a second. My pulse rate is 65 per minute by the clock. In a little over two pulsations the gust runs 60 feet, the length of the fence opposite. Count repeatedly, and find it a near approximation of 8–10 miles per minute, or 70 feet per second. This is prodigious velocity.*

"2 P.M.—Rain slackens, sky lightens up, but wind gusts are terrific; house shakes and trembles . . . a deep roar beneath the dashing, splashing and crackling noises around us." Through a rattling windowpane Forshey watched sodden dogs struggling through the water to reach the steps of his house. Pity outweighed caution and he shoved the door open against the wind and let the miserable strays inside. Then a horse clumped up his steps and rested wearily against the outside wall. "The air is filled with fragments and trash, the Heavens filled with portent. This is," he noted, "a genuine tropical hurricane, but the duration of the N.E. wind is inexplicable."

By 3 P.M. the rain had stopped, but the wind was still strong and the skies were black. With the water beginning to recede, Forshey ventured outside and saddled his pony

---

* Prodigious, indeed. Forshey's first figure would indicate a wind velocity of 480–600 m.p.h., obviously not possible; but 70 feet per second, or just under 50 m.p.h., is nearer the mark.

to explore the town. He found the Strand and the streets nearby littered with wreckage. Ships had been wrenched from their moorings and flung "away up streets and out on the prairie," wrecked or damaged. "It was difficult," he said, "and somewhat dangerous to reach the points I attempted, for the salt spray cut my face and blinded me and nearly capsized me and my horse in the flood. The bay and the harbor looked mad with turbulence and destruction. Darkness closed in upon me in the flood, and the storm raved on."

The hurricane blew itself out that night, and the morning of the fourth dawned bright and clear. The autumn winds, greatly diminished, blew fitfully from due north, but the noonday temperature reached 85 degrees. Forshey waded up the Strand until he reached an emporium known as Kahn's Building. There, Forshey "drove two nails in the west wall, inside, 13 inches above the floor to mark the high-water mark of the flood. With marking ink [I] inscribed along a black line, H.W., Oct. 3, 1867. Let this be remembered." But Forshey's high-water mark was remembered for a short time only; the true significance of his black line failed to ignite the interest of Galveston officials in seeking a way to defend the city against invasions by the sea. The million-dollar litter was scooped out of the streets, and Galveston baked in the sun.

Five years later Galveston was hit by storms six months apart. On June 4, 1871, a hurricane's periphery lashed the city carrying with it a measured rainfall of 15.57 inches, again flooding the ground-level floors and ruining thousands of dollars' worth of perishables. On October 3 of the same year the season's second blow drenched the town, and huge wind-driven waves jerked the S.S. *Hall* loose from her moorings, broached, and finally sank her with all hands aboard. Thus far, however, Texas's long white stretch of coast had been spared a hurricane's greatest scourge and mass-killer, the storm surge.

Over deep ocean, waves generated by winds exceeding 70 m.p.h. can reach the height of a five-story building; and beneath the center of the storm the ocean's surface is drawn upward, like water in a giant straw, to a foot or more above normal by reduced atmospheric pressure. Crossing the Continental Shelf, the storm can push in its vanguard a water level fifteen feet higher than the mean. This advancing surge is laid on top of the normal tides caused by the moon and, in turn, monster waves caused by the wind are superimposed on the whole gathering system. When the storm surge coincides with an incoming tide, the effect is calamitous.

South of Galveston, a hundred and twenty miles down the coast, lay the busy and pleasant town of Indianola, itself a port and railway terminus with a population of nearly four thousand. Indianola was sited at the head of a long bay, and behind the town there were so many smaller bays, lakes and bayous that the town was virtually an island. Like Galveston, the town's highest point of land was only a few feet above mean high tide. On September 16, 1875, a hurricane with winds estimated at higher than 100 m.p.h. tore into Indianola, and water, backed up by the winds to great depths, was driven seaward with stupendous force when the gale shifted direction. The town was crushed flat. Rescue workers sorted out the wreckage the next day and pulled 176 corpses into grotesque parade-ground formation for identification and hasty burial.

Indianola was rebuilt, but eleven years later, on the night

of August 19, 1886, an even worse storm fell on the town, the surge from the sea joining with the incoming tide to form a black wall of water moving with terrifying speed and unimaginable mass. Indianola, a toy city sitting almost at sea level, was backhanded out of existence. No building, house, stable, barn or bridge was left standing. Parts of the town were flung into the prairie, toward Port Lavaca, miles away, and in the lakes and bays behind the destroyed town floated splintered remnants of homes and the bodies of live-stock and human beings, bobbing obscenely in water still clouded by sand particles swimming in the residue of the storm current. The survivors picked through the debris, sal-vaging oddments of value, and moved inland with no thought of return. Indianola was to remain shattered and abandoned, a ghost town mouldering by the sea.

To every anxious caller at the other end of the telephone line that Friday, Cline could only say that the storm would be upon them rather sooner than later and that they would be wise to choose their high ground well in advance. *Should we*, many of them asked, *flee the island altogether?* This was a difficult question to answer. Relative safety can be reached by moving as far inland as possible as quickly as possible, but this presupposes access to rapid transportation and advance warning; there was little enough of the latter, and by no means could everybody afford the price of round-trip train tickets for entire families and the concomitant expenses involved in travel up to a hundred miles. If, as was then the case, the heading and forward speed of the storm mass could not be determined from hour to hour, migrating east or west on foot, horseback or mule-drawn wagon to escape the hurricane could just as well mean blund-ering into the center of destruction. The decision to run or to stay were made according to degrees of fear or optimism within each individual, emotions influenced largely by wind and weather prevailing at the moment. Although Cline had warned against being "fooled by today's sunshine," such is human nature that only a handful of families opted to seek shelter inland. The others could not realize the decision to trust in God and their own good luck was literally one of life or death.

Late Friday afternoon Isaac Cline guided his buggy purposefully along Galveston's beach front. His rakish white broad-brimmed hat was pulled down against the 13-m.p.h. wind blowing, he noted thankfully, from the north and against the incoming waves that boomed ashore with increasing thunder. Despite a thermometer reading of 90 degrees he was, as usual, spiffily dressed in frock coat, stiff white collar and a carefully drawn neckpiece partially hidden by the neatly trimmed Van Dyke. He reined up to watch a long heavy swell heave up out of the Gulf and undulate along the length of gray horizon to come sweeping ashore in a foaming curve that reached far past the usual tidal penetration. Nowhere, Cline reflected bitterly, had the city been successful in erecting a concrete barrier against even abnormal swells, much less against killing storm surges. Money had been forthcoming from the Federal Government to build and maintain the hugely expensive jetties designed to upgrade Galveston's status as a harbor and to increase national, state and corporate revenues—but none could be badgered out of any treasury to begin work necessary to protect lives and property. Calculations revealed with saddening clarity that the money spent on the jetties would have been enough to build a concrete seawall sixteen feet thick girdling five miles of the city's vulnerable coastline.

But not even Indianola's dreadful lesson was tocsin enough to stir the various treasuries to action.

Six weeks after the destruction of Indianola, thirty of Galveston's most powerful businessmen, calling themselves The Progressive Association, gathered to discuss the problem. These were men who were largely responsible for Galveston's booming prosperity, and saw in the steamrollering of the port town to the south a clear warning that Galveston was wide open to the same fate. The meeting ended with the issuance of a public resolution calling for the speedy construction of a seawall to protect the city's future. The resolution was applauded by the *Evening Tribune* in a front-page editorial. "When men such as these say that work on seawall protection should be commenced at once and pushed to completion, the public can depend upon it that something tangible will be done—and that without unnecessary delay."

But the *Tribune* was wrong. Money and energy would not be forthcoming for another fifteen years, and by then it was too late.

In a contemporary explanation, a former city engineer for Galveston named E. M. Hartrick said, "The people of Galveston will go on living in fancied security as they always have. The plan was perfectly feasible. Just after the storm [at Indianola] I drew plans for a dike ten feet high extending completely around the island, except for the north side. There, the wharves were to be raised to form the dike. The city gave the plan consideration, and the legislature later gave authority to bond the city, but this was some months after the flood, and by then the attitude was, Oh, we'll never get another one—and they didn't build."

Failure to provide Galveston with either the most rudimentary defenses or any kind of disaster plan lay almost entirely with the woefully inefficient city government, which had not changed its essential character since 1839, sixty-one years before the rising of the storm. The city was run by a mayor and a dozen aldermen who were supposed to serve the needs of the people living in the town's arbitrarily drawn twelve wards. Originally, aldermen were voted into office only by those living in the particular ward the alderman was to represent, but this system produced so much factional strife and outright vote-buying and pressuring it was abandoned in favor of elections at large. This was a step in the right direction, but failed badly in obviating the original evils of personal gerrymandering. For all intents and purposes, Galveston was a two-class society. A political expert from New York delved into Galveston's socio-political structure and came up with an interesting analysis.

Reported George Kibbe Turner, "The character of the population of the city discloses the fact that there is a very large number of laborers residing here. One-fourth of these are Negroes, and a large number of the remainder are foreign-born. You have a large number of saloons, and saloons usually participate in politics. I also find that there are a great many merchants and bankers in Galveston, but the middle class, the backbone of every community, is the smallest in proportion to your population of any city that I have yet visited."

Lack of a voting bloc made up of a middle-class backbone resulted in an indifferent selection of aldermen who served neither the interests of one class or the other. One of Galveston's progressive-minded middle-class citizens, E. R. Cheeseborough, commented: "We have never had a dishonest mayor, but our greatest trouble stems from the boards

of aldermen, their political jugglery, their caucuses and endless speechmaking." This jugglery produced budgets that
consistently exceeded income, resulting in annual deficits
of never less than $100,000. Every two years the state legis-
lature was asked for authority to issue $200,000 in floating-
indebtedness bonds to meet the recurring overexpenditures,
and as city taxes were not due until October of each year,
the city was further forced to borrow anywhere from $50,000
to $100,000 to tide the city over during the summer months.
The upshot of all this financial sleight-of-hand was that city
bonds were quoted at the lowest figure in history, interest
payments were not being met, and by the summer of 1900
there was no money in the treasury for current expenses;
instead, scrip was being issued in lieu of cash, and since the
scrip was heavily discounted the expenses mounted. Thus,
on the eve of the storm, Galveston was on the verge of
bankruptcy as a corporation, despite the fact that it was, per
capita, one of the richest cities in America. In short, Galveston was a pauper wearing ermine.

As Cline stood on the beach, a lonely figure with his
hand clapped to his hat, carefully timing the increasingly
heavy swells, he could see Galveston's densely packed
structures, the mean and the magnificent, ranked like
phalanxes of tenpins—and not one building stood on ground
higher than 103 inches above the level of the sea. The slope
of the long curve of beach stretching off to the west was so
smooth and gentle that even small children negotiated it
with ease.

Galveston was a besieged fortress without walls, keep, or
moat.

# Chapter 4

# RAIN IN THE MORNING

THE FORWARD QUADRANTS of the hurricane passed across the 90-degree meridian, on a line with New Orleans, and swept straight ahead as though locked on rails. On this heading the storm was bound for Corpus Christi, near the mid-point of the deeply curving coastline that begins at Port Arthur and ends at Brownsville on the Mexican border.

The system of destruction spread darkly across the periphery of the horizon and towered upward to blot out the sky. Torsion winds strong enough to snap telephone poles whirled around the hollow eye, a narrow shaft of calm in an otherwise violent atmospheric world. Years later, man would penetrate into the heart of such awesomeness and describe what is found there:

"Through bursts of torrential rain and turbulent bumps, then suddenly . . . dazzling sunlight and bright blue sky. The eye . . . surrounded by a coliseum of clouds whose walls rise vertically on one side and are banked on the other like galleries in a great opera house. The upper rim, some seven miles high, rounds off smoothly against a blue sky. Below, a floor of low clouds rising to a dome eight thousand feet above the level of the sea. There are breaks in the dome, giving glimpses of the surface of the ocean; in the vortex around the eye the sea is a scene of unimaginable violent, churning water."

Outside the eye at a radius of forty or fifty miles the tearing winds rip into the ocean to generate waves as high as a three-story building; surging upward they fell back like the collapse of high scaffoldings, creating deep and roiling valleys. Sometime after midnight Friday, this immense structure of nature's insensate fury altered course a few degrees to the north; only a few, but enough to point the vortex just left of center of Galveston.

Shortly after dawn Saturday, real estate agent and insurance broker Buford T. Morris rose from bed and walked across the floor to his bedroom window. Morris had his offices in Houston but spent his weekends in Galveston in a house he had built at Mechanic and 14th Street, on the eastern edge of the business district. He pushed the curtains aside and looked up at the sky. Morris later remembered, "The sky seemed to be made of mother of pearl; gloriously pink, yet containing a fish-scale effect which reflected all the colors of the rainbow. Never had I seen such a beautiful sky." The Impressionistic scene soon altered to leaden gray, and Morris was forced to bring down the window when the first heavy drops of rain began to fall.

Galveston stirred itself to the accustomed Saturday morning routine. Ike H. Kempner, one of the city's more affluent men, left his house on 20th Street and walked to his office through the slanting rain. Kempner was on time to keep an appointment with a businessman named I. H. Kemp, who had arrived the night before from Wichita Falls in northern Texas. The subject of the conference was water; Kempner was interested in the problems involved in irrigating the high plains region to assure a continued flow of water for the crops even during periods of drought. As the meeting went on, rain slammed against the office windows Kemp, the inlander, grew concerned and queried Ike Kempner about the possibility of Galveston being caught in the vise of the storm. Kempner reassured the other man, pointing out, "We have had storms before. Most of our homes are built on high stilts and the water has never come up into them. Then, too," added Kempner, "Commodore Maury, the famed oceanographer, recently issued a statement to the effect that storms originating in the West Indies area would not place Galveston in their natural paths."

It was now raining harder than ever.

Ruby Credo, twelve years old, sat before the large breakfast table with seven of her brothers and sisters and listened while her mother and father discussed the ominous weather that had grown around them since the day before. The

Credos lived six blocks from the beach in a "comfortable French-style two-story house with storm shutters, large porches and a picket fence all around." Although the edge of the Gulf was several hundreds yards distant the Credos could easily hear "the long, roaring swells breaking on the shore." Ruby Credo, like other children her age, was excited at the prospect of being in the middle of a real storm. And since today was Saturday, she wouldn't have to be in school and miss everything.

When Anthony Credo finished his breakfast he put on his hat and went off to work, just as he had done on every Saturday for as long as Ruby could remember. He told his family that there wasn't anything to be alarmed about, because "this storm will be just like the ones we have gone through before."

Ruby and the other children went outside to play in the narrow front yard, but their attention was drawn to the direction of the Gulf and the sight of "pounding waves and spray going up into the sky." Rain began to fall, and the children hurried underneath the shelter afforded by the wooden porch. From there they continued to watch the anger of the sea. When the waters of the gulf flowed toward them without receding, when the sidewalk disappeared under an incoming wave, Mrs. Credo opened the screen door and shooed everybody inside.

By 10 A.M. the wind had risen to 24 m.p.h., with gusts to 30, and telephone wires began an eerie rising and falling singsong along the length of the island. Inside the B'nai Israel synagogue, an imposing limestone structure with minarets and vaulted windows gazing at the heart of town, wiry little Rabbi Henry Cohen listened to the drumming of water against the slate roof and reflected upon the wisdom of cutting the service short so that the congregation could go home early. Because it was the Sabbath, Cohen's "regulars" inside the temple walls were among the few in Galveston who stayed dry during that Saturday morning.

Outside, the spectacular confrontation between the familiar beaches and the fury of the sea was a magnet that attracted thousands of thrill-seekers despite the soaking skies. One witness remembered that "many went out in their best bib and tucker to see a sight that was grand . . . beautiful . . . awe-inspiring. Well-dressed men and women disembarked from the streetcars at the beach and picked their way amid swirling pools of water and the spent waves to get into the Midway and to pass along to places where a good view of the sea could be obtained.

"For a few minutes they succeeded in keeping feet and bodies reasonably dry, but . . . umbrellas counted for naught and were soon turned wrong side out or ripped into ribbons. The owners abandoned themselves to the inevitable and went around seeing the sights, caring not for the weather nor worrying about their good clothes. Some, with abundant foresight, appeared on the scene in bathing suits and of course were right in it from the jump."

Crowds were heaviest along a tawdry ten-block stretch of beach known as the Midway, a crowded section of ramshackle frame boxes housing merchants catering to the souvenir tastes of weekend visitors. Here were sold seashells, garish postcards, salt-water taffy, kewpie dolls, satin pillows and cheap copper ashtrays; hot weather sharpened the reek of boiling clams, frankfurters frying in their own grease, of mustard, beer and brine; the air, during the long summer days, was alive with delighted shouts of swimmers, shrill cries of seabirds and strident exhortations of the penny arcade hustlers, all rising above the gentle and monotonous crash of Galveston's famous breakers. Dominating—almost overwhelming—the Midway were three enormous wooden structures run out over the water on trestles and floating high in the air on myriad piles. One was a three-tiered circular arena used for dancing and moonlight band concerts, and from a distance it looked like a wedding cake for a giant. The other two buildings were bathhouses of great proportions, especially the twin-domed "Pagoda," fully two blocks long. Splashed along the sides of these Brobdignagian pier-vaulted closets were messages from the M.K.&T. Railway: "A Ride on the Katy is Like a Drive on the Beach"; and, "The Katy to Klondike."

Ranked like so many cars awaiting loads of cattle or wheat were portable bathhouses, on wheels, that were trundled into position on the beach every morning to receive their human cargoes. These gaily painted wagons were among the first structural victims of the storm. The crowd gasped and aaahed when they watched the houses "picked up by the great waves and dashed against the row of flimsy structures along the Midway and piled up against them in uneven stacks." The waves rolled in almost on top of each other, smashing against the black and barnacled pilings supporting the monster bathhouses, but these creosoted poles planted deep in the sand seemed to hold. Onlookers watched the high rolling breakers sweep so near the Pagoda's flooring that it seemed that a rise of only a few more inches would punch up the boards and send spray flying through windows and roof.

Although the downtown streets were beginning to layer with water falling from the sky, this did not keep the streetcars from operating what amounted to an excursion service. Cars returning from the beach with soaking wet but exhilarated sightseers quickly filled again with those eager not to miss the excitement. At times the waves leapt over the trestlework near the beach, and conductors, fearful of shorting out the motors, were forced to discharge passengers more than a hundred yards away from the tumult. The fresh gawkers nonetheless slogged their way through ankle-deep water, pushed along by the wind, to reach the Midway area where, incredibly, a number of concessionaires stubbornly remained open, still hoping to extract final nickels and dimes from the remnants of the summer trade.

The holiday atmosphere among the curiosity-seekers was not apparently dulled by the sight of the waves wrenching loose the stairways and platforms leading from the beach to the bathhouses. Quickly reduced to shapeless debris, the planks were tumbled in disarray along the length of the beach. The platform supporting a quick-print photographic studio at one end of the Pagoda began to sway. The pilings were loosened in the sand, and when one monstrous wave rose to crash against the studio walls, the whole complex collapsed into the sea. Here was direct evidence of the storm's power to destroy, yet the crowd lingered. Later in the forenoon, when the incoming waves undermined the streetcar tracks along 24th Street near the beach, the cars stopped running. Some of the more prudent sightseers turned back for town, and few of them failed to notice how much harder it was to make headway against the wind than it had been only an hour before. But none seemed to realize that the storm was not an entertainment, but an executioner.

On the other side of the island, the normally tranquil bay

was turned into a cauldron by the heavy wind out of the
north that chopped the surface into serrated and fast-mov-
ing walls of water that slammed repeatedly against the
wharves. Spray shot into the air, where, mixing with the
rain, it fell in thick sheets upon the dockworkers who struggled to service a half-dozen ships waiting to receive or discharge cargo. At 11 A.M. the sloop *Cora Dean* wallowed
drunkenly through the rough and swollen waters of the bay
and made secure. By then, the water had risen to the level
of the wharves and no further navigation was possible; the
*Cora Dean* was the last vessel to enter Galveston that day.
The elements had gained the upper hand; shipmasters and
longshoremen gave up the struggle. The port was closed,
the workers left for their homes, and the sailors returned
belowdecks to ride out the storm.

Despite heavy weather, with winds and rain worsening
hourly all along the upper Texas coast and into western
Louisiana, the trains continued to run, filled with those who
had made travel plans for Galveston days and even weeks
earlier. A. V. Kellogg, a civil engineer, had business in Galveston that Saturday, and in a driving rain boarded a Galveston, Houston & Henderson coach in Houston and took
his seat for the usual ninety-minute run. As the train moved
slowly across the dual-tracked long bridge connecting the
island with the mainland, Kellogg noticed that the waters of
the bay were only two feet beneath the level of the tracks.
The train made it safely across the bridge and started moving for Galveston, but was stopped by a frantically waving
signalman who said that the track upon which the train
stood was washed out farther ahead. What about the Santa

Fe tracks that ran parallel to their own, he was asked? The signalman replied that the Santa Fe tracks were still firm, but he could not guarantee for how long. It was decided to wire for a relief train to come out from Houston on the Santa Fe tracks, transfer the passengers, and push on into Galveston. Kellogg's train remained where it was for an hour and a half, and he watched uneasily as the water continued to rise, covering the rails entirely so that the train seemed to be floating on top of a lake. Then the train backed up five hundred yards to meet the relief train on higher ground. It was now past noon, the winds were higher than ever, and it was obvious that the storm had yet to approach its full fury. There was still time to return train and passengers safely to Houston before the long bridge was swamped or blown down, but the passengers wanted to continue the slow, wet and windy journey to Galveston proper, now much nearer than the security of Houston nearly fifty miles away. Trainmen donned rubber boots and got out to slosh ahead of the engine, clearing the tracks of large pieces of driftwood and other flotsam, and thus the train was ushered into the Santa Fe depot at 1:15 P.M.

While Kellogg's train was inching its way across the bay, another rail drama was being enacted only ten miles distant. Coming from Beaumont, Texas, eighty miles northeast of Galveston, were two coaches and a locomotive operated by the Gulf & Interstate Line. Aboard were nearly one hundred passengers and crew, many of whom had made connections at Beaumont out of New Orleans. The train had left Beaumont early that morning in foul weather, which only worsened as it made its way south, then west along a flat spit of land known as Bolivar Peninsula. At the tip was Bolivar Point, where the steam ferry *Charlotte M. Allen* was to take the train aboard and carry it two miles across the bay to Galveston Island.

One of the passengers, John H. Poe, a member of the Louisiana State Board of Education, watched as the ferry fought its way toward the slip through sheets of rain. The ferry seemed to be standing still in the water, and when the captain tried to bring her around while maneuvering for the slip, winds broadsided her and she lost way. After several futile attempts the *Charlotte M. Allen* turned about and made for Galveston, leaving the train still on the tracks with water covering the wheel hubs and rising fast. The conductor lost no time in getting underway, and the train started backing for Beaumont

Many of the passengers, Poe among them, had cast longing glances at Bolivar lighthouse standing about a quarter of a mile away. Of iron and concrete and standing almost a hundred feet high, the lighthouse beckoned as a haven away from the howling winds and surging water and blown spray that coated the coach windows with a film of approaching death. Poe and ten others, including two women, hurriedly grabbed their bags, jumped off the slow-moving train and started wading. The train backed out of sight, soon lost in the downpour. Poe never expected to see any of the passengers alive again.

# Chapter 5

# FORCE TWELVE

A WEATHER BUREAU OFFICE, like the bridge of a ship, must be efficiently manned during a crisis. But the weatherman, unlike a ship's captain, can seldom take action or avert disaster; he can only stick to his post and tend to his instruments for posterity's statistical benefit. Cline's outpost atop the Levy Building had been fully staffed since 5 A.M., both shifts overlapping in order to keep the island and the nation advised of the progress of the approaching disaster.

Besides Cline, there was his brother, Joseph L. Cline, and a newcomer named John D. Blagden, a temporary replacement for one of Cline's regular observers then on a ninety-day leave. Blagden, whose home was in Memphis, Tennessee, had volunteered for the Galveston assignment two weeks earlier and had arrived in Galveston in time to place himself in the center of what was developing into the worst storm of his long experience with the Weather Bureau. He picked up a pen to record the 2 P.M. readings, oblivious of the continual ring of the telephone—now answered by Dr. Cline, now answered by brother Joe, now answered by himself—as monotonous and as predictable as the ticking of the big government clock hanging on the wall. Blagden noted that the barometer was sinking rapidly, now down to 29.37, two-tenths of an inch down from the 7 A.M. reading, and he knew that it was going to plummet to disastrous levels. The wind had already shredded the storm flags, and he could look out of the window and watch water creeping into the main streets.

Cline, after another wet excursion to the beachfront, returned to the office to send a telegram to Chief Moore in Washington.

UNUSUALLY HEAVY SWELLS FROM THE SOUTHEAST. INTERVALS ONE TO FIVE MINUTES. OVERFLOWING LOW PLACES SOUTH PORTION OF CITY THREE TO FOUR BLOCKS FROM BEACH. SUCH HIGH WATER WITH OPPOSING WINDS NEVER OBSERVED PREVIOUSLY.

The last sentence was ominous indeed, and the weathermen shuddered to think what would happen if the winds shifted direction and began moving with the incoming waters from the Gulf.

There were neither telephones nor time enough for the increasingly anxious townspeople to find out from Cline's office what the next hours were likely to bring. With salt water now covering the southern part of town, the early excitement had turned into apprehension. When the huge Pagoda bathhouse was torn loose from its pilings by winds and smashed to splinters by mountainous waves, the thick crowd of thrill-seekers melted away toward homes and hotels. Now many of them appeared at the door of the weather office, drenched and frightened, to ask what they should do. "Move to high ground," Cline told them, "because the worst is yet to come." This was slender advice, but there was no more that could be offered.

In Galveston, "high ground" was a relative term. The lowest surveyed elevation was 2.3 feet, at 9th Street where Avenue M almost ran into the sea. But the average, citywide, was 4.5 feet, a differential of little more than 26 inches. Galveston's spine was Broadway, laid down on a ridge that sloped gently down to both sides of the island. Even here, the maximum height above sea level was only 8.7 feet, at 15th Street, dipping down to just above 4 feet twenty blocks west. These small differences in height were certainly not discernible to an untrained eye; judging elevation was made impossible in any case by the density of houses packed tightly inside every block. High ground? There didn't seem to be any.

Nevertheless, approximately a thousand homes were evacuated, and as many as six thousand people began making their way toward the center of the island, seeking shelter in the stronger-looking houses. Doors were opened everywhere, and it is interesting to note that afterward there was not a single complaint of being turned away because of being black, poor or foreign; people who had never dreamed of entering one of the Broadway "mansions," except through the service entrance, found themselves invited to sit on brocaded silk seats of Louis Quinze chairs and offered coffee poured from English silver pots. Houses built to accommodate a family of six or a dozen were filled with thirty or forty, most of them strangers. In a city where there were thirty-six churches, and in a time when religion was a meaningful part of most middle-class Americans' lives, there was no embarrassment when some patriarch stood among those gathered in what was hoped was the strongest room in the house and said, "Now let us pray. . . ."

Less than half of those living in the threatened areas near the beachfront opted to leave. A rationale was given by a long-time resident of Galveston, a man who knew the temper of the people. Explained Clarence Ousley, editor of the Galveston *Tribune*: "Many were unafraid or judged their houses sufficiently strong. There had been high waters before, notably in 1875 and 1886, when the effect was mainly discomfort and wrecked fences. For years the physical geographers had argued plausibly, supported by experience, that the high-water records were the maximum of possibility because the beach at Galveston slopes so gently to the ocean depth that destructive waves would be broken and their force would be dissipated before reaching the shore. Thus assured, many a man of intelligence and ordinary prudence surveyed the rising tide with perfect equanimity. The inundation would be wasteful and damaging, to be sure, but it brought no danger to high-raised and stoutly built houses, had no terrors for self-possessed and reasoning persons."

Among those who judged his house sturdy enough to withstand the full force of the hurricane was Dr. Cline who, after ten hours in the office, was persuaded to return home to see about his two daughters and his pregnant wife. When he arrived the water was waist deep in his front yard, and

The Queen City offered white and tree-shaded havens from the heat of a subtropical sun. Tall windows captured every Gulf breeze, and iron gates were open to those who earned wealth from the land and the sea. (*Rigmor Mason*)

Energetic pioneer Michel
Branamour Menard, a
French émigré, founded
Galveston along modern
lines in 1838. Latecomers in
an affluent society were
content with modest cupolas
and riots of wooden gingerbread in homes intended
for large and exuberant
families.
*(The Rosenberg Library)*

Menard's own home, which he called The Oaks, was a simple
structure ordered from Maine and shipped to Galveston in sections
aboard a square-rigged bark. Walter Gresham eclipsed every private
structure in town with his Broadway palace furnished with crystal
chandeliers from Venice, damask from London and marble from Rome.
Built of limestone, sandstone and granite, Gresham's towered monster
was designed to withstand the siege of time and nature's furies.
(*Rigmor Mason*)

Turrets were borrowed from an earlier European culture and were used in Galveston as observation posts peering at the flow of commerce. These adorned the storied, thirty-roomed mansion built by R. S. Willis in 1894. The town blended lacy elegance with stone grandeur, watched over by medieval griffin. *(Rigmor Mason)*

William Lewis Moody believed in the continuity of a city's manifest destiny. Reverend James M. Kirwin placed his faith in God and in massive cathedral walls. Weatherman Isaac Monroe Cline (seen here in later years) sounded the tocsin against disaster sweeping from a maddened sky. (*The Rosenberg Library*)

Today the National Weather Service's network of radar stations provides surveillance of Atlantic and Gulf hurricanes. This is Beulah as seen on the radarscope at Brownsville, Texas, in 1967. (*NOAA Photo*)

The wasteland that was Galveston after the wind and waters of assassination returned to the sea. Survivors stand near the debris of what, only days before, had been a neighborhood of unpretentious homes facing streets filled with children's laughter and the soft murmur of summer's breeze. Through shattered downtown streets tiles flew like shrapnel, killing morning wanderers. *(The Rosenberg Library)*

Belgians shipped half a million bricks to inaugurate building of Sacred Heart church. Fifty years later, hurricane winds shredded brick walls and toppled two-ton bell then sounding the Angelus. Statue of Mary, Star of the Sea, withstood the assault. Interior of St. Patrick's church, seen as a refuge, became instead a tomb for uncounted and unknown faithful.
(The Rosenberg Library)

Freakish gales often left one building standing sound and whole,
while scraping clean its neighbor's façade. The rubble below was all
that remained of Lucas Flats. Torn by wind, battered by wreckage
of homes that had disintegrated earlier, the apartment building
collapsed upon itself, killing almost everyone sheltering inside.
(*The Rosenberg Library*)

Sanctuaries that withstood hurricane better than most others were medical building familiarly known as Old Red, and St. Mary's Infirmary, below, where those struggling in the angry waters were plucked to safety through windows by hardy nuns.
*(The Rosenberg Library)*

Human salvage operations were undertaken throughout the storm. Artillery troopers fled the beach to take cover inside nearby Denver Resurvey School, but the storm's cannonade caused heavy casualties.
(*The Rosenberg Library*)

No part of the island was spared. These cars, loaded with goods for markets of the world, were splintered by massive wall of water sweeping Galveston from end to end. Perversely, only the Deep Water Saloon survived. Rosenberg Avenue Public School, not far from town's center, was gutted by wind, collapsing floors, but desks bolted firmly down failed to slide into the rubble. *(The Rosenberg Library)*

the flooded streets were filled with people looking for a place to weather the storm.

Meanwhile, Joe Cline was struggling through the streets in the business district, wading in water four feet deep and battered by 50-m.p.h. winds. He managed to reach the telegraph office, where a final message was to be sent to Washington saying that the Gulf was rising and that water covered "about half the city." This news, based on the 3:30 P.M. observations, was nearly an hour old and, as Cline saw on the way from the Levy Building, was hopelessly wrong: water now covered *all* of the city and was rising at an alarming rate. His trip was wasted anyhow; he reached the telegrapher's desk only to discover that the lines had gone only minutes before. Cline hurried out of the building and back into the gale. Had all the telephone lines gone, too? When he reached his office he learned that there was still a single line open to Houston, and over this he gave the final—as it turned out—report to Western Union, there to be relayed to Chief Moore. Shortly afterward the telephone lines were blown into the bay and Galveston was cut off from the mainland.

In the city room of the Dallas *News,* three hundred miles to the north, editors stood around a suddenly dead telegraph instrument. Fifteen years earlier, the Galveston *News* had established a sister journal, the two papers connected by direct wire. And now, for the first time since 1885, the connection between the Dallas daily and the "Old Lady by the Sea," as the Galveston paper was called, was broken. Terse messages had been coming in all morning, each one more ominous than the last; then they ceased abruptly. Had Galveston been swamped? Were their colleagues now dead, lying crushed beneath the ruins of the *News* building? At the moment the line went dead, City Editor William O'Leary was in the office of the Dallas manager, G. B. Dealey, showing Dealey in the famous Commodore Maury's Geography "that the destruction of Galveston by tropical storm could not happen." The Dallas telegrapher could not get a current report on Galveston either from Beaumont or from Houston. He then tried Vera Cruz, Mexico, for there was a cable linking the two towns, but Vera Cruz reported no contact with Galveston, now a completely isolated—and for all they knew, a dead—city.

Anyone who has ever been caught in the blast of wind blown backward by the huge metal propellers of commercial aircraft engines will have an idea of the ferocity of the winds that hammered at Galveston during the morning and early afternoon. But as the stylus on the barograph continued its disastrous sinking with the onrushing approach of the storm's center, the winds increased to gale velocities. Small trees, their grasp on the earth weakened by inundation, were uprooted and flung away; shutters were ripped away and sent flying into houses nearby or blocks away; lightning rods were torn out of sockets and were fired like javelins through the sky. At five that afternoon the barometer stood at only 29.13, and the wind reached 74 m.p.h., Force Twelve on the Beaufort scale, true hurricane.

Up in the weather office, John Blagden waited for the windows to blow in. He was alone, having persuaded Joe Cline to return to his brother's house where he boarded. After all, the office had been useless as a communications center since the wire went down, and Blagden said he would stay with the instruments. At 5:14 P.M. Blagden recorded 84 m.p.h. on the wind gauge, and three minutes later the anemometer on top of the building was ripped loose from its substantial moorings by a gust of wind Blagden could estimate at from 100 to 120 m.p.h. Cut off as he was, Blagden could only wonder at what might be happening outside the walls of the Levy Building.

Through the black and flooded streets groups and individuals struggled for survival. There were those who had too long delayed their decision to reach high ground and there were those whose flimsy houses had already vanished into the maw of the storm. As they struggled in the darkness a new horror rose in the winds. After the great fire of 1885 an ordinance had been passed requiring all of Galveston's homes to replace the inflammable wooden shingles with tile. And now these tiles were pried loose by the wind and whirled through the air like so many heavy razors, striking into the soft carapace of human flesh with the impact of shell fragments. Caught in the open, scores were cut down by these missiles that whizzed in the darkness, and decapitation was not uncommon.

The thousands who placed their trust in God and in their contractors by remaining in their homes now faced their great ordeal. The great enemy had always been water that rose at predictable rates, ruining carpets and soaking everything not moved to the second or third floor, but winds that were now assaulting the city were never dreamed of, nor their force understood. Winds of 150 m.p.h. exert a force of one hundred pounds per square foot; thus an exposed wall measuring twelve by forty feet would have a total pressure exerted against it equivalent to twenty-four tons. Only those structures footed in solid foundations and made of brick or reinforced concrete can withstand such pressures, especially after foundations have been soaking for hours and battered by previous winds. And in Galveston such houses were not the norm.

Stanley G. Spencer, a well-known Philadelphia realtor with an office in downtown Galveston, was among an incredible number of businessmen who had so little regard for the progress of the storm that they kept their offices open until late in the afternoon, at an hour when the streets were brimming with water, the electricity was gone, and houses on the lower end of the island were coming apart plank by plank. Spencer had received one of the last telegrams into Galveston, a message from the home office in Pennsylvania asking him to meet with a realtor named Richard Lord. Spencer called Lord and suggested that they meet at Ritter's Cafe and Saloon, a well-known watering place on the Strand. Ritter's was housed in an all-brick building, and Spencer said that it would be a safer and certainly more pleasant place to discuss property exchange than any place he could think of.

Spencer, Lord, and "a Greek named Marcleitis" were seated at a table discussing business and, as witnesses remembered, making jokes about the storm raging outside. One man called out, "Hey, Spencer! I've just counted, and there are thirteen men in this room." Ritter's was located on a street leading directly to the wharves and was receiving the full blast of the hurricane winds; the howling was so loud that Spencer had to shout back his reply. "You can't frighten me," he said with some jollity. "I'm not superstitious."

Then the roof of the building was torn away and the ceiling under which the thirteen were sheltered collapsed, bringing down with it several printing presses and heavy beams, crushing Spencer, Lord, and a man named Kelner. Others saved themselves by diving under the heavy oak bar that ran the length of the room. Besides the dead there were five others who were badly injured, and Ritter ordered the black waiter out into the storm to find a doctor. The waiter, whose name went unrecorded, made his way through the door and into the maelstrom only to be knocked off his feet and sucked under the water to drown a few blocks away. Inside the shambles of the saloon, the uninjured scrabbled among the debris, trying to reach those whose cries of pain were inaudible in the roar of the wind funneling into the roofless building.

Those who watched the gutting of this modern brick structure as though by artillery fire now realized what Galveston's wooden homes faced from then on, until the hurricane blew itself out.

Little Ruby Credo was surprised to see her father come home so early in the afternoon; after all, when he had left the house that morning he had told them the storm would be like the others. Now Anthony Credo, his clothes soaked through, gathered his large family together and said that he had walked part of the way home with Dr. Cline, who said he was worried more than he liked to admit. Credo told his children to get ready to walk uptown to higher ground while there was still time. Then Credo and his wife grabbed an axe and a crowbar and began chopping holes in the parlor floor and prying up boards to let in the rising water and so keep the house from floating away. This done, the Credos called for the children; but before they could leave, two neighbors appeared at the door and asked for shelter. Old Mrs. Theodore Goldmann and her son, Will, explained that Mr. Goldmann stubbornly refused to leave his own house, but that if the others wanted to take shelter with the Credos it was all right with him. By the time the mother and son had been outfitted in dry clothes and given hot coffee, the water had risen too high and was running too fast for Credo to risk trying to get everybody uptown.

In back of the main house Credo had built what he optimistically called a storm shelter, a small one-room house built on six-foot poles and covered with latticework underneath. Credo decided the children would be safe there, and one by one he swam them through the backyard and into the shelter. From his own back porch he could see houses closer to the beach coming apart like blotting paper. He plunged back into the water and retrieved the three children and got them back inside the house. Ruby Credo, to whom so far the hurricane had been the most exciting thing she could remember in all of her eight years of life, recalled:

"The water was rising rapidly to the second floor, so Papa helped us climb from the outside through dormer windows to the attic bedrooms, where Mr. Goldmann and his mother had moved. The water had risen so fast Mama hadn't time to grab her cherished black satin corset from downstairs.

"We were drenched and all I could find dry was a petticoat. We stood at the windows and watched the houses around us break up, wash away, and become battering rams to knock and tear others apart as they were hurled and swept about. The water kept rising; the sounds of the storm were frightening; the house creaked and groaned as if it were in some kind of agony."

When darkness fell Ruby Credo was sitting on a corner of one of the beds, opposite Mrs. Goldmann and son. Suddenly the roof was split apart by a short section of streetcar rail that was washed, or was blown, through the shingles. The rail crashed inside the room, miraculously hitting no one, but the house was doomed; they could feel the house moving on its foundations.

Credo's wife was pinned to the wall when part of the roof caved in, and to free her he was forced to strip her of clothing, using parts of it to bind up gashes in her head. She was hardly freed before the house lifted from its foundations and began floating on the waves. Credo got his family out of the attic windows and into the water, but the Goldmanns simply disappeared and were never seen again, nor was Mr. Goldmann, who perished a block away.

"When our house left the ground," Ruby recalled, "we grabbed at anything washing by, as Papa had instructed us to do, but it was all you could do to stay on a piece of wood. The waves would shoot way up into the air and force us apart from the debris we were clinging to. Papa would raise his body between waves and tell us what to do next. The waves washed us north, then took us back south. We would separate, then come back together again. My brother, Raymond, was struck in the back of the head by a floating telegraph pole and knocked unconscious, bleeding badly from a deep gash. Papa struggled to keep Raymond's head above water, but several times he almost let him go because Papa was becoming extremely tired. Papa thought Raymond was near death, or dead already, but Mama refused to give up hope.

"An upside-down roof floated by and with great difficulty we managed to crawl aboard, being careful that it didn't crash down on us as it rose and fell with the waves. Mama and my sister, Florence, helped Papa pull Raymond onto the roof, but Papa got on some other debris nearby, not wanting to risk swamping us.

"The rain whipped by the wind felt like bullets hitting

our bodies and I didn't like the beating and pelting my back was getting, but I forgot about the rain when we realized that our roof was breaking up. A much sturdier porch floated by, and we got on that. The porch had been tossed upside down and was supported by heavy timbers underneath, and we each had a two-by-ten-foot section to cling to. Queeny, one of my older sisters, was in the middle of Vivian and Ethel, and they were holding each other's hands and clutching at each other's clothes. We floated this way for about an hour, then a piece of timber blown up by a wave struck my three sisters a terrific blow, knocking Vivian into the water and under heavy debris. She was quickly lost to sight."

The Credo family rode the wildly bobbing porch for hours. Exhausted, the children fell asleep in each other's arms, awakened only by shouts from their father that he saw lightning in the skies; lightning, he said, meant that the worst of the storm had passed, that the water would soon subside. Behind them, in the darkness, Credo could hear fragments of conversation from a couple like themselves drifting on some piece of wreckage. There were sharp cries of pain from the woman, who was in the early stages of labor, her condition made worse by a fractured leg. The Credos listened helplessly to the shrieks from the wife and the hopeful words of the husband until the porch drifted against an intact two-story house and lodged there. Credo led his family across yards of flotsam to reach the upper floor, where they were welcomed by the owners and given clothes and food. Moments later, the couple who had been floating behind them piled up against the same house and the injured woman was delivered of her first child by unskilled hands.

Credo had seen one of his children die, and in other parts of town two grown daughters, a son, a son-in-law and four grandchildren were killed. Nine dead in all, but Credo was later to consider himself lucky that so many of his family had survived.

Like Credo, William McIlhenny found himself struggling for survival on a roof with his family, but the roof was his own. Water forced him to lead his wife, five members of the family, and the visiting five-year-old son of a friend up on the shingles. They clutched at each other and grabbed for fingerholds where the tiles joined while winds tore at their clothing and rain and spray blinded them. A jagged piece of timber was lofted onto the roof and struck McIlhenny's small boy, Haven, tearing him from his father's grasp and bowling him into the waves. Surging water curled across the top of the house, carrying away first the Rice child, then McIlhenny's eldest daughter and her youngest son. A wind-driven plank knocked his other grandson off the roof and into the cauldron. Now McIlhenny and his wife were alone, clinging to the shingles, separated only by yards that might as well have been miles. The house shuddered from the beating it was taking from the waves, but the foundations held. The roof did not; winds tore at it under the eaves and wrenched it away, spinning it into the water where it broke apart in two sections—McIlhenny on one, his wife on the other. He watched helplessly as his wife's part of the roof slowly capsized, dragging her underneath the water not to reappear.

Thus did McIlhenny watch his entire family die one by one. Hardly caring, he continued to hold on to the fragment of his house until, eight hours later, an ebbing tide left him beached miles away.

Not many in Galveston faced the hurricane alone and lived to chronicle their experiences. One who did was Dr. S. O. Young, Secretary of the Cotton Exchange, whose observations reveal a presence of mind verging on clinical detachment. Young, an amateur meteorologist, had made a chart of the storm system for his own amusement and for the edification of his friends four days before the hurricane reached the island. Young's forecast, done on Tuesday, was for the storm to "strike somewhere near the mouth of the Mississippi." By Saturday morning, he realized that his chart was worthless, and he dashed down to the telegraph office to send a message to his wife, then en route to Galveston with their children aboard a train, to lay over in San Antonio until the storm had passed. It never occurred to Young to try to get out of Galveston himself: "I felt satisfied and very complacent, for I was fool enough not to be the least afraid of wind or water." When Young returned from the telegraph office he dismissed his young black servant and set about preparing his house for the onrushing storm.

He locked every door and window, got out candles and kerosense lamps, anticipating electrical failures, then dragged a comfortable armchair near an upstairs window facing south and prepared to watch the progress of the hurricane as though he were a spectator at a football game. Young's two-story frame house, on Avenue P½, was set on brick pillars four feet high, and although he was a bare two blocks from the raging beachfront it never occurred to Young that he might be in danger.

Through the rattling windowpane Young watched "the water as it flowed down the Avenue at a terrific rate, carrying wretched shanties, boxes, barrels, wooden cisterns and everything else that fell in its power. The debris fairly flew past, so rapid had the tide become. At 5:40 P.M. there was a marked increase in the violence of the wind. I went to a west window to watch a fence I had been using as a marker on the tide, and while I was looking I saw the water rise four feet at one bound. A few minutes later several houses on the south side of Avenue P½ went to pieces and floated away."

Young returned to his easy chair and continued to gaze outside until thumping noises from a first-floor bedroom prompted him to get up and go to the top of the stairs. He was astonished to discover that water was lapping against the final treads, only inches away from his feet. Young now began to consider the possibility that his house might not be invulnerable, after all. He made his way to a door leading to the second-floor porch and opened it. He was immediately blown back into the hall by a terrific blast of wind, but by keeping his back against the wall and maneuvering slowly, he regained the door and hauled himself outside, pinned against the wall by the wind.

"The scene was the grandest I ever witnessed," Young remembered. "The roar was something awful. I could see to the left and to the right, and only my house and that of my next door neighbor, Mr. Youens, were left standing, and we were practically out in the Gulf of Mexico. About two minutes after I got out on the gallery I saw Youens's house begin to move forward. It turned partly around and then seemed to hang, as though suspended. The wind switched to south-by-east, and Youens's house rose like a huge steamboat and was swept back and suddenly disappeared. I knew that he had his family with him—his wife, his son, two daughters—and my feelings were indescribable as I saw them go."

Young watched without panic as the shifting winds drove the swollen Gulf onto the porch where he stood, thirty-one feet above the ground, and began pouring into the upper hallway. Uprights and porch railings ripped loose and were sent flying. A post struck Young, gashing his head and turning his shoulder numb. He held on to the door facing, a plan working in his mind for when the house was uprooted, as he now knew it would be.

With the supports gone, the porch roof blew away over the top of the house. After this the porch floor simply floated off, leaving Young flattened against the house, suspended in air with one foot inside the door. "It was an easy thing to stay there," he explained, "because the wind held me as firmly as if I were screwed into the house." Looking inside the flooded hallway, Young was transfixed by one of nature's phenomena. "The drops of rain became luminous as they struck the wall; it looked like a display of miniature fireworks. The luminous particles were about the size of pinheads, but one ball about half the size of a boy's marble formed on the door facing and slowly slipped down into the water."

When the wind reached maximum force Young calculated in his head that his body offered five square feet of surface to the blast and that he was being subjected to a pressure of 590 square pounds. He was suddenly impatient for the house to tear itself loose from his own sore structure. "I began to think it would never go, but finally I felt the house yielding. I took a firm hold of my door facing, placed both feet against the house and exerted full strength. The facing tore loose, and as the house went I kicked myself away from it as far as I could so as to avoid sunken debris rising to the surface.

"The house rose out of the water several feet and was caught by the wind and whisked away like a railway train. I was left in perfect security, free from floating timbers. The water was almost flat, beaten down as it was by the wind, and there was not even the suspicion of a wave—but the current was terrific. Almost before I felt I had started I was floating over the Garten Verein, four blocks away, and at the next moment I was at the corner of the convent. Here I got into a large whirlpool and caught up in heavy debris. I was carried around and around until I lost my bearings completely and was then floated off (as I found out afterwards) to the northwest, finally landing in the middle of the street at 34th Street and Avenue M, fifteen blocks from where I had started."

Young floated on his door facing for more than eight hours. Although he was almost precisely in the geographical center of the city's residential area, all he could see were the tops of a few houses and the wreckage of others. During the entire time Young heard no human voice save that of some unknown woman feebly calling for help. After a while the cries stopped, and Young was left alone, believing that he was the only survivor in a part of town housing thousands of people. Wracked with chills and giddy from loss of blood from the still-open head wound, Young was not sure he could last the night. He bobbed around for hours, and when the water subsided he waded to an elevated cottage and was sheltered by fifteen or twenty Negroes "who forgot their own misery when they saw me bareheaded, covered with blood and shaking with cold."

The Reverend Judson S. Palmer had moved his family from Sharon, Pennsylvania, to Galveston in order to escape the brittle cold of Eastern winters. Now he faced an enemy he had never encountered before, a berserk sea flooding his living room and climbing for the top of the stairs. Palmer gathered his wife and only child in his arms and said prayers for them all, then listened as the small boy, Lee, added, "Dear Jesus, do make the water go down and give us a nice day to play tomorrow." The water swept across their feet, and Palmer with nowhere else to go, herded his wife and son into the bathroom in a corner of the top floor. When the water rose above their chests the Palmers managed to climb onto the edge of the old-fashioned bathtub. Palmer held his son on his chest while his wife clutched at the shower fixture overhead. The water came up to Palmer's neck and he knew that they were all going to die unless some miracle occurred. At that moment Palmer felt the house shift and begin to topple. His feet left the bathtub edge, the ceiling became a wall, he felt his grip on his son loosen and his wife's arms slide from his neck. Then water covered his head and Palmer hoped that drowning was quick and painless.

He came to and found himself on top of what seemed to be a bundle of shutters torn from the house. His wife and son had disappeared, and he shouted for them until he was hoarse and salt water gagged him into sickness. But no answer came. Where his house had stood there was only debris flung about in the waves. Palmer's raft was slammed into a shed and disintegrated. He swam feebly until he reached the roof of an outbuilding of the Catholic convent. He stayed there until the water went down and the sun began to rise. It would, after all, "be a nice day to play," but Palmer never saw his wife or his child again; the miracle he had hoped for applied only to himself.

In a small one-and-a-half-story house at the corner of

19th Street and Avenue O½, not far from where Reverend Palmer's house stood, William H. Irvin knew when faith in the integrity of his house must be abandoned and trust in blind luck begun.

Irvin, his wife and their eight children crowded the modest home, but when five neighbors, including three youngsters, fled from their own frail houses seeking refuge they were readily admitted. Irvin was not concerned about the increasingly violent winds, for his was the strongest house in the block; but foot by foot he and the others were forced to retreat up the stairs by the surging water until, finally, he led them into the attic, the last redoubt. From the darkness outside they could hear the anguished cries of those whose houses had already been knocked to pieces. There were a dozen people jammed into the attic and the close confinement coupled with the sounds of terror only yards away created a sense of entombment among them all.

Irvin himself felt acute fear when his own house began to sway back and forth, accompanied by an orchestra of creaks and groans as the sturdy timbers began to loosen in the joints. When the sway worsened and the first cracking sounds began, Irvin knew what he had to do. He grabbed one of his older children and heaved him out of the attic window "to land," as he said later, "I knew not where." One after another Irvin's children were jettisoned into the black unknown. Then he pushed his wife through the window, followed by the neighbor's children, their mother and Miss Aldridge. Then Irvin grabbed the window sill and propelled himself outside.

He landed heavily, not in deep water as he had anticipated but on a broad expanse of wooden roofing. Amazed, Irvin discovered that the eleven others who had preceded him were all aboard the same raft—the top of a backyard storage shed jerked from its foundations to lodge against the house just underneath the attic window. Irvin reached in the water for a plank and pushed the shed clear of the house. The heavy current carried them away before the house tipped over, the roof coming apart in a shower of wood.*

Robert L. Johnson was one of the relative few who had no confidence whatsoever in the ability of his house to withstand the onslaught of a hurricane; it was the typical two-story wooden structure built on Avenue S, and too close to the beach. Like many others, however, Johnson had lingered at his downtown office in the belief that the storm would be more nuisance than threat. He quickly changed his mind when the bay overflowed the wharves and began flooding the business section. When debris began to fly through the air Johnson quit work and started for home, twenty blocks away, to fetch his family to higher ground. Before he reached his front door he was "forced to wade in water up to my neck."

By the time he had readied his wife and three children for the attempt to find a safer house to ride out the storm, water was already bounding into the upper floor and Johnson decided it was too late. He looked out the window in time to see his neighbor's house, only fifteen feet away, come apart and go down in the booming waters carrying, Johnson assumed, all five members of the family. Down Avenue S came two small cottages, tipped this way and that in the current, stopping momentarily when they smashed up against a telephone pole. "I heard women and children

---

* The shed held together, but two children, one of them Irvin's, were later killed outright by flying slate or timber. Irvin's wife was fatally injured and died a few days later. All of the others, however, survived the floating ordeal that lasted until the following morning.

screaming," said Johnson, "and the words *Oh, God, save me!* rang in my ears."

The two cottages floated on down the avenue, bound for the sea, replaced by three others in the macabre parade of death. Johnson knew the houses and the occupants—the Artizan, Henman, and Jennings families, eighteen people in all—and as the houses rushed past his own he could see forms struggling in the water. Johnson, who believed it was their turn next, reached to kiss his wife and children good-bye. As he did so, his eldest boy, fifteen, looked up and said with conviction, "Father, it is not our time to die."

The mood was heightened by "the piercing scream of a woman, followed by a crash, and another house turned over on its side and was driven past by the wind and the flood, the current running like a mill race. The water was already on our second floor and the waves knocked us about until we were exhausted."

But the house held, against all Johnson's expectations. When the worst had passed he looked out upon the once crowded neighborhood and saw that his was the only house left standing within a two-block radius in a wasteland of destruction. Still, something seemed odd to Johnson: later measurement showed that the wind and the water had nudged his home off its foundations and moved it forward ten feet in the sand without cracking a timber.

The more sparsely settled western end of Galveston was cut off from the rest of the town early in the storm, deepening the sense of isolation felt by those living miles from the center where it was natural to assume help lay, where rescue efforts were surely being organized, where there was the precious extra two or three feet of higher ground. The people who lived "out there" assumed they were getting the worst of it and had no way of knowing that the pattern of death and survival was the same all over the island.

Henry R. Decie, his wife, and their child lived eight miles west in a poor house that had not the slightest chance of absorbing more than a minimum of the punishment then being dealt all around. He walked his family through four feet of water to his nearest neighbor. They were seated at the foot of a bed in an upstairs room when a tide of water swept the house off its blocks. Mrs. Decie threw her arms around her husband and cried into his ear, "Good-bye, Henry, we are gone!" The house caved in and Decie found himself in the current, paddling with one hand and gripping his young son with the other. Decie looked down and saw that a piece of falling timber had crushed his son's skull. He gently cast away the small corpse and grabbed for a floating beam almost the size of a telephone pole. The current carried him northeast across the island through bouncing heaps of wreckage. Something smashed down and broke his left hand. Bobbing timber reared up and struck him in the face. Blinded first by blood, then by grotesque swelling that shut both lids, Decie thereafter lost track of where the current was sweeping him. Decie banged around in the water for the rest of the night and was finally flung ashore near Cow Bayou, thirty miles from Galveston.

Another long-distance rider was sixteen-year-old Anna Delz, whose house was near the western beach. "Together with a girlfriend who was staying with me I packed my mother's trunk and carried all the household goods that I could and piled them in the second story to keep them from being washed away by the water.

"At around 4 P.M. my mother and my sister, who was thirteen, were taken by a friend to a place of refuge, but my girlfriend and I were left at home in the belief that we would be safe. But not an hour later the house went down with a crash and myself and the others were thrown out into the furious waters. I caught on to a tree and hung there for awhile, [but] when a roof came along on which there were about twenty women and children I got on and stayed with them. They were washed off one by one until only another young girl and myself were left. Then she was gone and I was left alone to battle the waves."

When the roof began to break up, Anna Delz waited until a substantial piece of timber came alongside, then she plunged into the water and hugged the beam with both arms. At first the erratic current swept her into the Gulf, then she was carried across the island past people struggling to stay afloat on driftwood like herself, past people floundering for something to hang onto, past lifeless forms lying face down in the water, until she was carried into the bay. By now Anna was not only bruised and exhausted but suffering intensely from cold; piece by piece her clothing —shoes, blouse, skirt, stockings and underwear—had been stripped from her body in the frantic scramblings from one piece of flotsam to another. The timber to which she clung seemed to grow heavier and harder to handle. When it drifted underneath one of the ruined railroad bridges crossing from the island to the mainland she cast it loose and clung to one of the pilings, the top now barely above water. The rough surface scratched at her bare skin but she could not recall feeling the pain. After a while she grew too numb to hang on, so she got aboard another piece of driftwood and let it carry her where it would. Hours later she bumped into a pile of lumber interlocked by the force of the storm and apparently in no danger of coming apart. She managed to climb on top and lie down, uncaring about her nudity and fell into an exhausted sleep.

The wild ride had carried Anna Delz eighteen miles.

The brick, steel and concrete heart of Galveston's business district was being torn to pieces by violent winds and the cannonading of heavy airborne debris that acted like projectiles hurled by twelfth-century siege engines. The W. L. Moody building, standing foursquare on the Strand with one side facing the open bay, was fully exposed to the 100-m.p.h. blasts of wind. Onlookers who had taken shelter in buildings across the street watched as the tin sheathing on the roof ripped loose and sailed through the air like crumpled paper. Then the entire fourth floor disappeared in a shower of red bricks "as if it had been sliced off by a cleaver."

The City Hall, symbol of Galveston's civic pride, towered above all the buildings around it, nearly 140 feet from base to center pinnacle rising above a massive clock. Turreted, adorned with statuary representing man's virtues, built of massive limestone blocks and elegantly narrow, the building—architect Alfred Muller's self-proclaimed masterpiece—was submerged up to the sills of the second-floor windows and looked like a ship fighting its way through heavy seas. The City Hall, for practical as well as psychological reasons, was a natural refuge, and as many as a thousand people packed its upper two floors to ride out the storm. Because it stood higher than any other structures for blocks around, the building was unprotected in any way.

The windows blew in, scattering shards of glass among the crowds on the second and third floors. Hurtling timber and whole sections of destroyed buildings smashed against the upper stories; one of the turrets was thus torn loose from the façade to crash into the street. Holes were punched in the roof, giving the wind purchase along its entire length. It came loose with terrifying sounds, pulling most of the third-floor wall with it, and those who had not managed to escape to the second level were blown through space to plunge into the water fifty feet down.

What was left of Ritter's Cafe came apart and was hurled against the back wall of the *News* building, smashing in the brickwork and letting in a torrent of floodwater. The Grand Opera House caved in, tearing down with it the top floor of the adjoining Grand Hotel. Inside the massive and ornate Harmony Hall, once the center of Galveston's Jewish social life but now an annex of the Galveston Business College, Professor E. P. Smith assured his wife and five children that they would come to no harm. When the storm began Smith had decided to flee from their house on 35th Street because the Gulf was less than a hundred yards from the front door. He had been teaching at the Hall for some years and knew it to be one of the strongest buildings in downtown Galveston; he was sure that the water could never rise above the high-ceilinged first floor. In this Smith was correct, but the force of the wind that uprooted lesser structures and sent them barreling through the air was beyond his imagination. Weakened by repeated blows from just such debris, Harmony Hall's multi-ton roof collapsed and buried all seven members of the Smith family in a corner where they had gathered to avoid the rain blowing in through the empty windowframes.

Ten blocks away, at the eastern end of Broadway, stood Lucas Terrace, three stories high and the first all-brick apartment complex built in Texas. Among the financially well-off guests staying at the "flats," as they were called in deference to the Englishman who built them, were the Edward Quayles, who had arrived in Galveston only forty-eight hours previously. Quayle, a tabulator on the Liverpool Cotton Exchange, had come to the States to examine the workings of America's largest cotton port. Unfortunately, the rapid change of diet, time zones and climate between England, New York and the Gulf Coast disagreed with Quayle, and it wasn't until Saturday afternoon that he felt really well enough to go outside. But by that time the hurricane was lashing Galveston and Quayle resigned himself to another twenty-four hours of confinement. When he did leave the room it was in a manner neither he nor his wife could have imagined.

As Mary Quayle later remembered, it was shortly after 8 P.M. when her husband walked over to a window, hoping to be able to judge the extent of the destruction raging all around them by the light of occasional flashes of lightning. This may well have been at ten minutes past the hour, when John Blagden's barometer registered 28.53 inches, the lowest reading of the past two days, the lowest it would ever record at Galveston. As Quayle stepped in front of the window, the pressure differential between the inside of the sealed room and the outdoors equalized almost instantaneously. The glass blew outwards and Quayle was sucked through the opening into the blackness outside, not to be seen again. Mary Quayle's screams attracted the attention of a man next door, who guided her out of her wind-blown apartment and into his own. Wreckage was pounding against the building, and when the wall began to give way they fled to another apartment, but that one, too, started to split apart, admitting a flood of water. Mary Quayle's savior, a man named Jonathan Hale from Gloversville, New York, led her out the door and into a corridor filled with people struggling in both directions trying to guess which part of the building would go next. It was a form of roulette with life-or-death stakes.

The majority guessed wrong and were crushed or drowned as section after section of the fashionable building was battered into wreckage as shapeless as that which was causing the destruction. For nearly two hours Hale played the deadly game with the hurricane and the building's structural strength, until finally he and Mary Quayle cowered in a second-floor corner flat, the only one that remained. Unbelievably, the wind died and the water stopped rising and they were saved—they and only eighteen others out of nearly a hundred who were in the building.

Any civically organized attempts at rescue were put out of the question by the magnitude of the disaster overwhelming Galveston. But there are always a small number of individuals who seem to lie in wait for just such crises ready to exercise initiative, knowing that the reward for success and failure alike may well mean death in the end.

W. H. Plummer, a city police officer known to the town as "Captain" because of his long years spent at sea, was one such man. Plummer lived in a modest frame house at the corner of Church and 7th Streets, at the very eastern end of town. In Plummer's backyard, lovingly maintained, was his proudest possession, a fourteen-foot boat with much free-board, built in the manner of those boats used by Maine lobstermen and known as an "Eastern pod." Built for deep water and rough weather, Captain Plummer's boat inspired confidence just to look at it. The boat was fitted with four heavy, wide-bladed oars, and inside there were two airtight compartments, one forward and one aft. When Plummer waded home from police headquarters early that afternoon the boat was already afloat in the backyard. Plummer exchanged his policeman's uniform for rubber boots and an old oilskin slicker and ordered his two grown sons, both merchant sailors, to dress for foul weather and help him launch the boat into Galveston's streets.

In that end of town, inundated since the morning, there was no lack of those waiting to be taken off porches already awash, or those who were trying to wade to safety through water deeper than they could manage. In a thirty-to-forty-knot wind and fighting the cross currents that swept through the streets, Plummer knew that attempting to reach higher ground toward the business district along Broadway, more than a mile away, would be a waste of time if not impossible. He reasoned that the sensible thing to do was to pick up as many people as possible in one load and row them to the nearest shallow water so that they would have a chance to wade out of the path of the rising Gulf. One of those whom Plummer picked up, Claude Pond, volunteered to stay with the Captain and his sons for as long as the boat remained in action.

The boat was rowed past houses whose occupants stared blankly at them from windows, refusing Plummer's offer of help. The peril, they said, was not that great. Passing the same way an hour later the boatmen were forced to push aside wreckage of the now-vanished houses and floating bits of furniture and other possessions the drowned owners had not wanted to abandon. More than once Plummer went over the side with a strong tow rope in hand, helping to pull the boat along, directing the prow toward some desperate group. He was at times wading in water up to his neck and sometimes was swimming against the current. Heartbreak was often added to fatigue.

With a crew of four aboard, at least two of them constantly manning the oars, Plummer could not take aboard more than eight or ten passengers; this sometimes meant ferrying only part of a family to shallower water while the others stayed behind to wait for the boat's return. Usually Plummer would transfer the parents first, then go back for the children, reasoning that if the ever-changing level of the water swamped the shallow place the children would either be with him in the boat or on their own threatened porches. With the parents safely deposited and with orders to keep wading away from the Gulf, Plummer, Pond, and the two boys would row hard to pick up the smaller load. In almost every case the parents stood rooted to the spot where Plummer left them, disregarding his shouted and waved commands to move on. They stood transfixed, unable to overcome the natural instinct of remaining as close to their children as they could. Plummer could only watch and row as a surge of water, a booming wave, rose to cover the miserable figures and sweep them from sight.

Plummer and the others somehow kept the boat from swamping or capsizing during the hours they moved through the streets in their "sweep area," from 7th Street out to 1st, and on both sides of the island as far as they could navigate. By early afternoon Plummer had to abandon the tactic of ferrying survivors to shallow water, for there was none as far as he could see. Instead he began rowing his soaked and often terrified passengers to St. Mary's Infirmary, one of the few brick buildings on that end of the island. It was a matter of rowing up to one of the second-floor windows and having the passengers step from the boat directly inside the venerable building. Captain Plummer's house was directly across the street. On one trip to the infirmary he saw his house still standing against the tearing wind and the hammering of the water; the next time he passed that way his house had gone, the wreckage churning down the street along with the debris of a dozen other homes.

Plummer's voyages were numbered. Tired to the bone, Plummer and his hands fought the boat towards the infirmary carrying nine others. With the sanctuary only yards away a flying timber crunched broadside against the boat and it capsized in the roiling water. The air-tight compartments maintained their integrity and herculean efforts by the crew saw the craft righted. But six of the passengers, so recently rescued and so near to safety, slipped away and drowned. The streets were now so choked with lumber, poles and wires and the wind so high and the water so rough that no amount of will or muscle could prevail. Plummer and the others made the boat fast and then stepped through an infirmary window to ride out the storm. How many had they saved? There had not been time to count, but Captain Plummer later reckoned that it was around two hundred.

Pete Brophey was no sailor—he was a corporation court clerk, his craft was an unimpressive rowboat that rocked alarmingly even in calm water, and there was no one to whom he could ask for help in attempting the rescue of his aged and terrified parents. They were alone in Brophey's house, listening as the wind ripped loose tiles, shutters and trellises, watching the water seep in underneath the front door, feeling the house sway on its foundations. Brophey had dragged the rowboat up to the porch to protect it from the storm, and now he knew he was going to have to launch it into the storm carrying his mother and father if they were to have a chance of survival. Brophey did not think the house could remain upright much longer. He got the old couple into the boat and cast off into the whirlwind of water that flowed past the door.

Brophey's destination was the house of a friend two blocks down the street, a house stronger than his own. The boat slewed and pitched in the millrace, but Brophey managed to keep the prow pointed downstream. Progress was halted by clutching hands. A man, his wife, their children were in midstream, water foaming waist-high. Their situation was obviously desperate, but Brophey wondered if he could fit them all in without sinking the boat; on the other hand, the extra weight might make it more controllable. The children were gathered in, followed by the parents. The boat sank almost to the gunwales, but raced on down the street. As it reached the Cleveland house the boat swerved, filled with water and sank. Brophey and the other man heaved, paddled and jerked and managed to get everybody pushed inside the house. It took only a few minutes for Brophey to realize that he had led them all not to salvation but to a trap; the house was already rocking back and forth, porch supports were tearing loose and the world seemed to be tilting.

Brophey was braced inside a doorframe when the wind knocked the house on its face. He surfaced in a welter of planks and lath. Of his mother and father and the family he had pulled from the water and the others in the house, there was no sign. He climbed aboard what seemed to be an enormous raft made up of the wreckage of several different houses pushed together by the churning water. When the raft came apart Brophey leapt onto a floating roof to join a shivering, nondescript dog who managed to follow Brophey during the wild ride and several changes of accommodation that followed during the next ninety minutes.

Finally Brophey and the dog reached a sorry-looking house still standing in the water washing past 37th Street. Brophey poled and paddled and reached a window where pairs of black arms hauled him roughly inside. The dog scrambled after him, gaining the window to land on a floor crowded with refugees. Brophey passed out and came to the next day in a hotel room where he was cared for by friends. "Where is my dog?" he asked. Nobody knew, but Brophey swore to find it, declaring, "Never while I am living will it want for a rug to sleep on or a bone to chew."

Isaac Cline, who had expended so much calculation and energy telling others to seek higher ground, confidently observed the progress of the hurricane from inside his own house only a few hundred yards from the beach. "I had built my house," he said, "with special reference to possible hurricanes from the Gulf. I had made it, as I believed, strong enough to resist any storm that might come. The timbers were heavy, the attic braced. . . ." Because their chief weatherman had chosen his home as a family redoubt, neighbors saw in the house an ark that would carry them safely through the flood. They flocked to the front door, beseeching entry; Cline turned no one away, and those he saw floundering through the street he beckoned inside. Soon there were nearly fifty refugees sheltered under his roof, none of them realizing they had placed their faith not in Noah, but in an unwitting Judas goat.

With his pregnant wife and six-year-old daughter close at hand, with his brother Joe upstairs with his two older children, with every room in the house filled, Cline went to the front door and risked the storm by opening it a few inches so that he could see outside and make observations. Water flowed in the living room to a depth of eight inches and Cline had to keep his shoulder braced against the door to keep it from blowing in. Above the scream of the wind he could hear the creak and crash of timbers as houses along Rosenberg Avenue and Avenue Q went to pieces. Cline was still standing in the door "when the water rose suddenly four feet, reaching above my waist, before I could change position." Cline was swept backward, but men rushed up and they managed to get the door closed.

Within the next hour, Cline observed, the water rose an additional five feet, bringing the total tide in that area to approximately twenty feet. Yet the house remained firm on its foundations. But the storm surge that had not fazed the Cline redoubt nonetheless brought about its destruction; all the other houses in the vicinity were dismembered and converted into huge battering rams. The strong current, then running east to west, brought this deadly wreckage piling up east and southeast of Cline's lonely house, where it began to smash against the walls with terrifying sounds. The booming and splintering lasted for thirty minutes, then the house came apart.

Cline was holding his wife and child to him when the walls caved inwards and the roof settled on top of them. He felt the bodies of his family slip away. A blow on the head stunned him. Cold black salt water rose over his head and Cline believed it was the end. He opened his mouth "with the idea that water would enter my lungs and death would come quicker." Then his head shot above the surface through a gaping hole in the roof. Cline automatically put his hands out and grabbed. His fingers closed around his daughter's ankle and he pulled her clear of timbers and hauled her onto the roof. Upstairs, Joe Cline had taken the other children in his arms and leapt from a window and into the water. He managed to get them on the roof, and they crawled for the center. They shouted for Mrs. Cline, but there was no answer; she, and thirty-five others, had vanished.

"We drifted for three hours," recounted Cline, "and for two of them we did not see a house nor any person, except for an eight-year-old girl who crawled to us over the timbers. From the swell I inferred that we were drifting out to sea, then southeast and easterly winds pushed us back again. During the last hour our piece of wreckage knocked several residences to pieces, and while we were drifting we had to protect ourselves from flying timbers by holding planks over our heads. We had to be constantly on the lookout and continually climbed from one drift to another. Finally we landed three hundred yards from where we started. During that whole night I seemed to feel no fear. I suppose I was beyond it."

# Chapter 6

## SANCTUARIES

**N**UMEROUS INSTANCES were recorded of families fleeing homes for the house next door or across the street only to be forced out when the walls began to give, wading or swimming to another dwelling and having to leave that one to find another—until four or five possibilities had been exhausted and either they had to swim for their lives among the wreckage or the ultimate house proved able to withstand the bombardment by wind, water and drift. Those who were already inside one of Galveston's large and imposing brick buildings built especially to house and care for hundreds did not have to face the agonizing and often fatal decision of where sanctuary might lay. These souls merely made themselves as comfortable as possible and prepared to wait out the worst the hurricane could offer.

Rudolph Daniels, Dallas-based passenger agent of the M.K.&T. Railway, was in Galveston when the storm broke and was one of many who sought shelter in the Tremont Hotel, the city's finest, a relatively new five-story brick hostelry at Market and Tremont Street in the very center of the business district. He was just finishing lunch in a restaurant across the street when the wind rose to gale force, its frightening howl urging Daniels away from dessert and toward the Tremont's lobby. "The water in the street was three feet deep and full of telegraph poles, beer kegs, boxes and other debris. Many of the Galveston roofs were oyster-shelled and the wind tore them loose and they flew through the air injuring people and breaking glass, adding to the infernal bedlam of sound of the rumble of walls and the rattling of tin.

"People from blocks around were trying to make their way to the hotel; rescuers stood on the sidewalk and when a man, woman or child would come within reach they would be seized and dragged inside through air thick with spume and spray."

Not all of them made it. A salesman named William Van Eaton watched two women and a child struggling up the street in swift-running water only to lose their footing and drown.

The Tremont accommodated some two hundred paying guests, and as late as noon that day most of them were milling around in the lobbies in a state of excitement and exhilaration. A guest named Adelbert Beecher watched in amazement as the others "joked, laughed, danced and made

merry while death [was preparing] a carnival in less fortunate sections of town." The mirthful atmosphere was suddenly changed to one of morbid curiosity as the first injured
victims were hauled in off the street to stagger inside and
collapse. The flow of refugees increased as the hours wore
on, most of them ushered through the door half-nude, many
of them bruised and bleeding. When the front windows
started blowing in and salt water began creeping over the
porch and onto the lobby carpets, paying guests realized
sickly that they were threatened with the same destitution
that had overtaken those who had come in from the streets,
and those who had already skirted drowning or maiming
wondered if death was following them into the hotel.

By the time Tremont Street became unnavigable, an estimated eight hundred to one thousand people were inside,
sitting hunched on the stairs, lying in attitudes of defeat
and resignation in the corridors, backed against walls of
rooms, away from windows, and badgering Manager George
Korst for food, drink and candles. To A. V. Kellogg, who
had gone through the ordeal of the stalled train coming in
from Houston, "the vibration of the hotel was not unlike that
of a boxcar in motion." From different parts of the hotel
Kellogg could hear the groaning of the injured, the sobbing
of the terrified, supplications to God and to Jesus Christ
and fragments of hymns, atonally and raggedly rendered.
But—and this was a feature remarkable for its absence
throughout Galveston wherever crowds gathered—there
was no panic; a reaction that in any case requires an abandoning of faith and a place to run to. From inside the Tremont, there was simply no place else to go.

Water poured in through the door, and one man timed

the rise at one-half inch per minute. By 5:30 P.M. the floor of the great rotunda was flooded, driving those who were sheltering there up the stairs. With an unbelievable crash the sprawling skylight exploded downward, raining shards of heavy glass into the rotunda's recently vacated artificial lake. But the rest of the roof held, wreckage failed to batter down the walls, and after the water reached to midthigh in the lobby the storm had done its worst to the Tremont Hotel.

Captain W. C. Rafferty, U.S.A., was looking to his guns. Rafferty, commanding officer of Battery O, 1st Coast Artillery Regiment, was responsible for $3 million worth of Government property—land, quarters, stores and armament. His domain included more than twenty acres, beginning out at 45th Street and extending to the sea. Fort Crockett, funded during the Spanish-American War, was not yet completed; the men were quartered in temporary barracks and the officers rented houses in the town. However, the huge concrete casemates were finished, housing the long ten-inch rifle, eight ten-inch mortars, and several smaller-caliber rapid-fire guns ready, as a contemporary editorial explained, to protect "the great seaport, the artery through which the trade of a vast section of country ebbs and flows, the haven which would be sought by vessels of the Navy if hard-pressed in the gulf during time of war."

Captain Rafferty and a detail had been busy since early morning Cosmolining gun breeches and elevating gears, covering the actions with heavy tarps lashed securely, and stowing everything movable inside the casemate rooms. What could be blown away was now hidden from the wind, and the ruinous effects of salt-water corrosion would be held to a minimum. Beyond this, Army field manuals could offer nothing more in the way of defense against the primeval enemy, a malignant sea.

Where the guns stood an artificial hill had been created, elevating the works a good fifteen feet above sea level in order to provide a better field of fire and to give some protection against unusual tide levels. Even so, by 2 P.M. the waves that had already wrecked the beach pavilions at the other end of the island were foaming against the casemates and eating away the dunes that had been piled against the concrete fortifications. Behind them on either side, Rafferty could see houses being rocked from their foundations and collapsing when they toppled into the flooded streets. His own house was none too strong, and he summoned one man from the gun detail and asked him to make tracks for his quarters and bring back Mrs. Rafferty, the children and the servant girl. Rafferty watched the man go over the dune and into the current, pushing aside wreckage as he went. Then the trooper whirled around and disappeared under the water.

Rafferty dismissed the detail, telling them to head for cover; there was no more to do for the guns, nor could Rafferty help his men: survival was now left to individual initiative. Rafferty kicked off his boots and stripped to his long johns and plunged into the water, swimming, wading and fighting his way to his house. He improvised a raft and got everybody aboard and headed, not for town, but back for Fort Crockett. Rafferty guided the others up the sand and along the concrete carapace until he came to a steel door at the top of a short series of steps leading underneath the ten-inch gun. He pushed everybody inside, down the steps and into the shell-hoist room, a low-ceilinged confined area

lacking ventilation and light. Rafferty slammed the door
shut and they sat hunched on the concrete floor, listening to
the bombardment all around them. The walls began to sweat
and drops of sea water dripped from an unseen crack in
the ceiling. Would the newly laid foundations hold? If not,
Rafferty knew that the massive gun only a few feet above
their heads would plunge down and turn them into pulp.

Inside the frame and tarpaper barrack housing the non-
coms and enlisted men of Battery O, First Sergeant Hugh
R. George shouted to make himself heard above the wind.
"This building won't stand half an hour. I'm getting out!"
He told the artillerymen it was every man for himself; those
who wanted to stay, could, and he would lead the others to
the new, all-brick Denver Resurvey Public School building
only a few blocks away. A dozen opted to stay in the barrack, thirty others followed the sergeant outside. Three were
drowned within sight of the barrack, and the survivors
reached the school building to find the first floor already
under water. Two hours later water was up to the armpits
and a wall blew in, killing three of the soldiers. Again, the
sergeant said he was getting out. Fifteen men followed him
into the storm, swimming, clambering from one piece of
wreckage to another, trying to make their way to yet another refuge, but one by one they drowned—including the
First Sergeant—until all were gone except a private who
clung to a piece of roof that carried him all the way across
the bay and two miles inland, where he grabbed the center
section of a standing telegraph pole and hung on until the
water receded.

True to George's prediction, the barrack soon was bowled
over, taking with it seven men. Five escaped, one of them
riding a door out to the Gulf and back again, then westward

down the island and finally into the bay. Another found himself swimming alongside a cow paddling frantically away from the town. The trooper, by hanging on to horn and neck, managed to keep his head above water and eventually got the cow headed back toward Galveston. When they were near enough for the soldier to make it back on his own, the cow tired and sank beneath the waves. The soldier later estimated that his four-footed benefactress had nursed him along for three miles, coming and going.

The Raffertys waited inside the darkened concrete cocoon, feeling the heavy shocks ripple through the hill under the intense bombardment. It may seem that wind and water would pose little danger to reinforced concrete structures such as the one under which the officer had chosen to risk the lives of his family—but had Captain Rafferty been a physicist or an engineer instead of an artilleryman, he might well have decided to seek shelter as far away from the ocean as he could get. One cubic yard of water, enough to fill a carton only three feet wide and three feet deep, weighs seventeen hundred pounds, nearly a ton. Thus a wave fifty feet long and rising ten to twelve feet high—and such waves were common that day—would be hurled against anything in its path with a static weight of approximately a hundred tons. Structures at Galveston were further strained by the high loadings the surfaces carried due to increased wind velocities. The combined pressures exerted against the fortifications at Fort Crockett were more than the smaller turrets could bear; cracks developed, exploited by sledgehammer blows of tons of moving water. Concrete split off in large ragged chunks and toppled down the slopes. One of the cumbersome mortars wrenched loose from its mountings and rolled ponderously into the incoming sea.

Captain Rafferty thought their time had come when a wall of water slammed against the steel door. It swung open, admitting a flood of water that dashed against the walls and bounced back outside, sucking with it the servant girl, who had been sitting near the door. Rafferty leapt forward too late to grab the girl, but he managed to slam the door shut before any more water could come in; the rest of it drained downward through the opening in the floor that led to the shell room just below. The Raffertys stayed inside the damp and dark cell for hours, terrified, cold, hungry, but alive.

·The remnants of Rafferty's command, the eight men who stayed inside the school building, endured their own hell of dodging death by running from one threatened classroom to the other. An entire half of the roof was blown away; then the windward wall on the third floor disappeared, followed by the collapse of the other part of the roof; and finally the troopers were huddled in the only remaining sound room in the building. These men survived to later gaze in awe at the school that resembled the target of intense and accurate shelling by enemy ships of the line.

To the believers—and the terrified—it was natural to look for salvation from the storm inside one of the town's forty churches or other edifices associated with God's work on earth. This was especially true regarding Galveston's Negro population, to whom religion was an elemental life-force and not a conveyance for social or sartorial prestige.

Organized worship for the blacks of Galveston began in the 1840s on a three-shift basis; in the town's then-only church the white masters gathered for service in the mornings, the slaves occupied the pews in the afternoons, exiting in time for the seignoral class to move back in for evening worship. According to an aged former slave known to all as "Auntie Ellen Roe," it was her one-time master Gail Borden —chief customs collector, later city property agent and prime mover of a dairy fortune—who was responsible for creating separate-but-equal religious facilities on the island. Auntie Ellen recalled how the Bordens "trained her carefully as to body, mind and soul after buying her, at the age of seven, from cruel slave speculators who stole little children and sold them upon the block." In 1851, Borden secured title to a lot on Broadway, near the booming business district, and helped collect donations for a new all-Negro church. Ellen Roe contributed the first dollar, painfully earned by reciting perfectly her Sunday-School lessons, in which she was strenuously coached by Mrs. Borden and later rewarded at the rate of twenty-five cents per recitation.

This original church survived the Civil War, and in 1888 the congregation built a new brick building stuccoed inside and out. By 1900 there were fourteen churches catering to the spiritual needs of Galveston's Negroes, none of them as well built as the one at Broadway at 20th Street; neither stone nor stucco was used—only the familiar two-by-four, lath, shingle, tile and tin. They were lovingly painted in white to repel the fierce subtropical sun, but as places of refuge from great hurricanes they were flimsy bastions indeed. One by one, all fourteen were destroyed, carrying down with them uncounted victims, leaving the survivors literally adrift to fight their way toward houses of God that were built of sterner stuff.

But churches that withstood the storm's assault were few indeed, and many who fled one collapsing house of worship were killed at the altars of others. The Second Baptist

Church was lifted from its foundations and torn to fragments. The West End Methodist was blown on its side, the
steeple broken into fragments. The Third Baptist was uprooted and moved into the next block; minister, wife and
child vanished. St. John's Methodist kept its spire, but the
roof collapsed in a welter of beams to crush the interior.
"Old Trinity" stood a three-walled ruin, the south wall,
facing the bay, disappearing "like a curtain rolled suddenly
into space." Freakishly, the remaining walls were untouched. The litany of destruction continued until twenty-
two of the town's Protestant churches were demolished,
the remaining dozen battered but still recognizable for what
they were.

The Catholics were hit just as hard.

The cathedral of the diocese of Galveston occupied a full
half-block along Church Street near the center of town.
Facing this solid structure were Cathedral Hall and the pa-
rochial school attended by some three hundred children
taught by seven Dominican Sisters. Father James M. Kirwin,
a tall, lean figure who had served as chaplain to the First
Galveston Regiment during the Spanish-American War, survived the storm inside St. Mary's to tell what happened that
day.

"We began to feel the effects early in the afternoon. The
tin cornice work began to fly off the cathedral and the air
was filled with slate from church and school. High over the
cathedral stood the statue of Mary, Star of the Sea, erected
after the flood of 1875 as protection against the storms from
the sea. The immense tower began to sway with the wind,
the water rose higher and higher to enter the lower apart-
ments of the rectory, compelling us to seek refuge on the
second floor.

"The janitor came in and announced that the roof of the school had broken in and that a large section of the east wing had fallen. Crowds had by now begun to congregate inside the church and we feared that the tower surmounted by the immense statue of Our Lady would topple over, causing great loss of life. I saw a fine horse rushing down the street in the surging water, and as he reached the front of the rectory an immense beam from the building opposite fell and caught the animal, ending his career.

"The wind grew fiercer, and the creaking of the tower framework and the prayers of the people congregating in the church mingled with the deafening roar. The sexton rang the Angelus; it sounded not like a salutation of praise but a warning knell of death and desolation. Then, out from its iron bands and clasps was torn the immense two-ton bell, fortunately landing on the tower floor. The iron crosses topping the front towers were wrung from their fastenings and carried into the street below. The immense tower had yielded to the fierce onslaught of the wind and the retaining wall above gave way.

"The destruction of the church and rectory seemed imminent. The bishop informed the clergy and household gathered in the upper rooms of the rectory to prepare for death. Then the wind veered to the southeast and slate from the school roof began to cut through the rectory windows. Finally the wind began to decrease and the water to recede. Mary, Star of the Sea, remained on high to continue her protection."

On the western end of town stood an uncompleted dream. In the early 1870s the Very Reverend Lawrence Canon Glynn began to oversee the construction of St. Patrick's Church, later described as a "magnificent pile of Celto-

Gothic architecture." Surpassing anything in the South or in the Southwest, the church spire reached 220 feet into the sky, topped with a Celtic cross inlaid with gold. The vaulted ceiling of grained wood was pattern-cut by European craftsmen who as immigrants left signs of their skill all over Galveston. The sanctuary blazed with the colors of nine windows of figured stained glass, and the nave glowed with ten pieces of leaded stained glass, all in the shape of shamrocks evoking memories of Eire. St. Patrick's stretched from one street to another, its length not equal to the impressive, steel-lined tower that dominated the Galveston skyline. The church was thirty years in the building—the steeple funded and built only a twelvemonth earlier—and although the final architectural touches were still some distance in the future, St. Patrick's was a functioning church, the pride of the diocese, and, in the words of Father Kirwin, "a thing of beauty, a fit abode for the dwelling place of The Most High." Here indeed was a fortress against the storm.

But as early as 2 P.M. most of those who would have flocked there were discouraged by the slates singing thick through the air, deadly as bullets, and the astonishing sight of the great spire swaying this way and that. One of the huge iron-bound windows flew outward from the casing and shattered with prismatic fury. The heavy golden cross leaned, seemed to totter, stayed, moved in one direction and another, all the while sending vibrations down the length of the massive spire. Even laymen could imagine what would happen if that 220-foot mass of brick, steel, and concrete fell, and those who were caught out in the open hurried past the threatened church, steering clear of that ominous cross.

It was a tribute to the designer and his workmen that the

tower did not collapse earlier, offering as it did some ten thousand square feet of surface to the brutal winds. At 6:30 that evening, it fell, most of it into the water-filled street, the remainder crashing through the roof. The noise must have been awesome, but it might as well have happened on the surface of the moon; those who remained in the vicinity, and survived, afterwards recalled that the sound of the crash did not reach their ears through the howling of the wind.

With part of the roof torn away, the complete destruction of the steeply slanting covering of the nave occurred within minutes, leaving St. Patrick's a gutted shell housing tons of rubble. Father Kirwin observed that "walls, roof, ceiling, windows, columns, tower, bell, pews, pipe organ and oil paintings were now in one vast burial blent." Two altars and four of the small shamrock windows survived, and nothing else. It was at first believed that none in Galveston had sought shelter within the church, but some days later, under a baking sun, the nostrils of passersby unmistakably revealed that this was not the case. So deep was the wreckage that a month later the causes of the offensive odor were still unrecovered.

On the eastern end of the city, filling an entire block along Broadway and complementing the great homes there, was the Jesuit showcase, Sacred Heart Church. This multi-spired, many-columned, flying-buttressed, arcaded, heavy-stoned monument to man's vanity and pride in faith had only recently seen installed fourteen huge and costly stained-glass windows imported from Munich, and the Jesuit Fathers from the Province of New Orleans, under whose authority the parish operated, knew that as St. Patrick's Cathedral on Fifth Avenue was to New York, so the Sacred Heart was to all of Texas. Located in that part of town that was hit heavily

during the storm's early stage, Sacred Heart quickly filled
with refugees, as did the adjoining St. Mary's University.
The great bronze bell in the belfry of the west tower began
to toll early, the pull rope guided by no hand, the uneven
and frantic clangor wind-driven over some four hundred
souls already dispossessed of homes. Now some of these same
homes came for them in a grotesque tangle of wreckage,
borne along by the turbulent Gulf sweeping the island. The
south and east walls were butted down, glass began flying,
and the brown-robed Fathers piloted groups of people from
one threatened part of the big church to another.

Because the walls were broken in one section at a time
and because the massive roof cracked and fell piece by piece
in a random pattern, and because those inside enjoyed as
much luck as any others on that day, survivors far outnum-
bered victims. Hurtling bricks and falling stones maimed
fifty people; they were laid out in whatever dry and hopefully secure areas the religious could find. The injured cried
aloud for water, for food, for bandages, all of which were
quickly exhausted. With nothing left, then, to give them
comfort, the casualties lapsed into lethargy. "All were thank-
ful for their kind deliverance from tragic death," observed
a man of the church, "and with truly Christian spirit and
sweet patience they suffered in silence."

The bell continued to toll throughout the night and into
the morning. Inside the nave wreckage was piled twenty
feet high, and nobody could guess how many were buried
there.

Saturday, September 8, was the feast day of Our Lady's
Nativity, and all that morning Sister M. Elizabeth Ryan,
thirty-six, had been in town to market for dinner that eve-

ning. Sister Elizabeth, who had come to Texas from Ireland, worked down the island at St. Mary's Orphanage, home to ninety-three girls and boys ranging in age from infancy to early teens. Their isolation from society was made all the more complete by the remoteness and isolation of the home, three miles west of town in a lonely part of the island only beginning to witness occasional beam-raisings, and the scattered houses were meaner than the others at the east end. However, the double-winged orphanage was near the sea, the air was clean and tinged with salt, there was sunshine more than three hundred days in every year, and the Sisters —six from Eire, one from France, one from Mexico, another from Canada, and an Alsatian German—were kind if stern substitutes for parents many of the children had never seen.

Water was already filling the streets and slate had started to fly from the roofs when Sister Elizabeth decided to head back for the orphanage. She was inside St. Mary's Infirmary talking with Mother Gabriel, while outside waited the orphanage wagon and two of the older boys who had helped with the shopping. The venerable Mother Gabriel begged the younger nun to stay at the infirmary, where it would be safe, but Sister Elizabeth pointed out that if she failed to return to the children they would have no dinner. Gathering the black habit above her ankles, she waded across the infirmary grounds and got aboard the wagon. Mother Gabriel watched the wagon disappear down Post Office Street.

Somewhere between the infirmary and the orphanage Sister Elizabeth's wagon was swamped, or capsized, or crushed by falling masonry. Neither she nor her helpers nor the wagon nor the horse nor the food so carefully bargained for were ever seen again. It made no difference that the groceries failed to reach the orphanage in time, for within a few hours there was no one there, no one left alive to enjoy a feast in honor of Blessed Mary, Mother of Jesus.

The Mother Superior, Sister M. Camillus Tracy, at thirty-one, was one of the younger of the orphanage nuns. When the waters of the Gulf and the waters of the bay slammed together, cutting off any possibility of flight, she ordered all of the children into the chapel, the main part of the building. Then she sent the orphanage handyman, Henry Esquior, out to the back to bring in the clothesline. This was cut into sections, looped and tied around the wrists of children divided into groups of six and eight, the ends of the lines secured to the Sisters' waists. Thus, like mountaineers awaiting the fall of an avalanche, boys, girls, nuns and the workman, a hundred and one beings in all, crowded the chapel to pray. Mother Camillus led them in song, a zestful hymn much loved by the children.

> Queen of the waves, look forth across the ocean
> From north to south, from east to stormy west.
> See how the waters with tumultuous motion
> Rise up and foam without a pause or rest. . . .

When the sea water flooded the chapel the children were led to the second-floor girls' dormitory, away from the beach. For an hour they listened to the rise of the wind and the creak of the building, then they heard the crash of the other wing, the boys' dormitory, when it came unhinged from the chapel and exploded into fragments. The structure of the orphanage building, thus weakened, could no longer stand. In darkness, surrounded by a howl of demons, the small children gathered next to the familiar black cloth and were so clutched when the roof crashed down and the walls split apart. The building quickly disintegrated, collapsing upon itself, then was flung away. Everybody died, probably instantaneously, except three.

Not roped together because they were the oldest, Will Murney, Albert Campbell, and a Bohemian named Francis Bulnavic who spoke almost no English found themselves outside in the water when the roof caved in; Will Murney, thirteen, later said he believed he had crawled through a transom to get out of the building. Young Murney swam until he bumped into a tree uprooted by the storm. A few minutes later Albert Campbell, who was Murney's age, and the Bohemian boy, a year older, floated by and grabbed branches. Murney helped the others onto the trunk. They discovered lengths of rope tied to the tree and wondered if others had not used it as a raft before them. Will Murney, the strongest, helped the others lash themselves to the trunk, and they began a voyage lasting for a night and part of a day.

The tree was swept outward into the Gulf, then back again, becoming entangled in the masts of the wreckage of the schooner *John S. Ames*. For hours the waves battered them, and several times Albert Campbell cried out that he was done for. Will Murney told him to hang on. When the sun rose the boys managed to free themselves from the wreckage and let the current carry them back toward shore. They came aground far down the beach and struggled through the ruins until they reached a house that was still standing, where the people inside were still alive. Francis Bulnavic was to learn that his five brothers and sisters, living with a Galveston family, had all perished.

Of the many solid buildings in Galveston, St. Mary's Infirmary was not among those likely to withstand the full weight of the storm. For one thing, the building was at the eastern extremity of the town, where the island narrows between the Gulf and the bay—six blocks from one, only three from the other. The brick building, twenty-six years old, was not large, and its only protection was a neat white picket fence running along Market Street. And it was surrounded by a host of frame houses waiting to be converted into battering rams that would destroy buildings two and three times its size.

Early that Saturday morning, Father J. B. Gleissner, an infirmary patient, was allowed out of bed to say Mass for the first time in six weeks. He returned to his room in the northwest corner of the recuperative ward and gazed out of the window towards the bay at "sprays of waves ten and fifteen feet high; the rising sun behind them made them shine like diamonds. It was a grand sight."

A nursing Sister told Father Gleissner, "Just a little storm is doing this. We are here nearly thirty years, and the water has never come to our gate."

But the water came now, past the gate and up the steps and into the reception room. Gleissner got out of bed and looked out of his window. The bay had vanished in a whiteout of wind and rain, but he could see people in the streets carrying bundles and babies, heading for the infirmary. He heard a crash; the great stone cross on the roof had blown down, shattering the Sacred Heart statue. Now Father Gleissner realized he was afraid. He dressed and went into the corridors to see what he could do; they were filled with men, women and children of the neighborhood, many of them plucked from the water flowing past the entrance by courageous Sisters who stood knee-deep to haul them inside. They were soon driven back by the rising water, but the infirmary filled with refugees who made it on their own or were brought to safety by Captain Plummer and his sons in their lobsterman's boat. Before darkness fell, there were about five hundred people in varying stages of dress and undress jamming the confined hospital building.

Sister Joachim, her habit torn and wet, appeared and ran to a window overlooking the rear of the infirmary, where an older, wooden building housed fifty-odd distressed and aged women. The Sister had left her charges in order to secure drugs from the infirmary dispensary, but by the time the medicines had been gathered up the yard separating the two buildings was alive with debris and swift-moving water. She told Father Gleissner she should not have come, she should have stayed with the patients. Then she turned away to help with the mass of refugees inside the hospital.

It was just as darkness fell that they witnessed the collapse of the home. "Oh, God!" Sister Joachim cried. "My poor old ladies are all killed." And so they might have been had it not been for the initiative and the strength of a young staff physician named Zachary Scott.*

When Scott saw that the Old Ladies' Home was threatened with extinction, he dropped what he was doing and dashed across the yard through water flowing above his ankles. He burst inside the home and picked up a helpless old lady in his arms and waded back for the infirmary porch, where others relieved him of his burden. He immediately started on a return journey that would be repeated until the home was cleared of patients. Toward the end of this herculean effort, Scott was near collapse and was laboring through water up to his waist. The last few women were car-

---

* And father of a well-known Hollywood film actor of the same name, perhaps best remembered for his portrayal of the evil genius in *The Mask of Dimitrios*, (1944), with Sidney Greenstreet.

ried away while the building was coming apart, and Scott missed saving only two: a woman named Mary Sweeney, crushed to death while she sat in a wheelchair, and an unknown child. It was only later that Sister Joachim learned of Scott's heroism, such was the chaos inside the infirmary at the time.

The windows had all been blown out and rents in the roof admitted cascades of water. The electricity was gone and the only light available was a single candle somehow kept burning before a Sacrament. The water had risen to the level of the staircase, forcing everybody to the second floor. Sisters and novices were praying aloud. One, who had apparently lost faith in the building, had to fairly shout to be heard above the din, "Let us pray for the dying, because the building cannot withstand the fury of the storm much longer; we will all be crushed to death. Let us depart, Christian souls, out of this world." Refugees, many of whom had become separated from families still somewhere out there in the storm, wailed and berated themselves for seeking safety while others perished.

Father Gleissner moved among the sodden and terrified crowd holding before him the Blessed Sacrament. "Fear not," he cried. "Christ is with us, the same Christ who calmed the storm on the Galilean Sea." Gleissner got the nuns and the novices to singing, and they encouraged the others to join in the chorus of "Queen of the Waves."

A man grabbed at the priest's arm. "Put your hands on the south wall and feel what cracks are there," he begged. Father Gleissner plunged his hand into the water and discovered "cracks big enough to put my arm through." They drew back in time to avoid being knocked flat when part of

the wall caved in. But this was the final damage the infirmary was to suffer.

What saved the building from total ruin was the fact that
the homes that were smashed all around the area were carried past the infirmary buildings by the monstrous current
before the wreckage could fuse and batter at the walls.

Mrs. William Henry Heideman had never been in a more
hopeless position. Half-nude, eight months pregnant and
utterly alone, she clung to a cottage roof that was being
swept along in the direction of the town's center, away from
the wreckage of her home. When the house went down she
was flung one way, her husband and their three-year-old
son another. The roof bumped along in the torrent and
banged against a piece of wreckage. Mrs. Heideman slid
down the shingles and fortuitously landed inside a large and
lidless steamer trunk bobbing in the waves. She eased her
bulk around until the trunk seemed to balance, and she
gripped the sharp edges of the trunk with what little
strength she possessed.

Fortunately for Mrs. Heideman, the vagaries of the current carried her directly for the largest and strongest building complex on the island, the Ursuline Convent, occupying
four square blocks near the center of town. There were forty
Sisters there, members of the Order of St. Angela, an order
that had established a reputation for stubbornness and devotion to duty in the face of previous disasters, both natural
and man-made. During the series of yellow-fever epidemics
that raged in Galveston from its inception through the Civil
War and beyond, killing thousands, and in one year more
than 10 percent of the population, the nuns had their own

ranks decimated by the disease they sought to alleviate in others. During the first siege of Galveston during the Civil War, General Magruder personally offered the Mother Superior and her charges safe-conduct out of the combat zone before the firing began, but the offer was turned down. Magruder was told that the Sisters would stay where they belonged, inside convent walls, acting as nurses for the unfortunate wounded of both sides. Federal gunners aboard ships in the Gulf mistook the convent for a Confederate stronghold and the nuns found themselves under bombardment. A yellow shirt, the international sign for quarantine, was dug out of one of the student's trunks and run up the flagpole, and the shellfire ceased.

Ursuline Convent recovered and, in 1894 completed an immense new building on expanded grounds. "The Convent," said Houston architect Howard Barnstone, "was high Victorian Gothic at its most elaborate, expansive, colorful and romantic. The succession of arched and foiled windows, deeply recessed to create sharp shadows in the sub-tropical sun, glittered and the multi-colored stones and brick were an endless mosaic—a magnificence never before or since attempted in Texas. Here was a supreme monument . . . a very large building, isolated where it could be seen from a distance, and the carefully studied silhouettes were varied by towers and other skyline features to enhance its scale."

The convent was surrounded by a brick wall ten feet high, and much of the wreckage was fended off before it could invade the grounds to get at the buildings inside. The wall was finally hammered to bits and it was over the ruins that Mrs. Heideman's trunk floated at full speed. The ornately decorated ramparts loomed up and Mrs. Heideman could see figures standing at nearly every window, most of them

dipping long poles or casting ropes into the water, like fishermen. The trunk bumped up against the wall; poles and
arms held it secure long enough for Mrs. Heideman to be
laboriously eased across a second-story sill and inside the
convent. She was carried to the seclusion of a nun's cell to
await the coming of a new life or the end of the world.

In the courtyard outside, a man clung to the branches of
a tree. Debris, swimmers and lifeless forms swept past his
feet. His name was Heideman, and he wondered what had
happened to his pregnant sister-in-law and the rest of the
family. The cry of a child drew his attention downward
and he swooped his arm into the water barely in time to arrest the flight of a small boy being carried past in the current.
When he pulled the child up to his level he saw with as-
tonishment that it was his nephew, last seen being cast from
the Heideman house blocks away. Volunteers from the convent managed to get both out of the tree and to the safety
of Mrs. Heideman's cell. No one would argue that a convent
was a likely place for the occurrence of a miracle of coinci-
dence.

Four blocks south of the convent the house of the James
Irwins went to pieces, and husband and wife watched each
other drift away in separate directions. Irwin fought his way
aboard floating lumber and was carried to the convent walls.
When workmen pulled him inside Irwin was destitute of
clothing and was provided with the nearest covering at
hand, a burlap sack. Even then, propriety was a consideration, and a hunt was carried out for something with which
to blanket Irwin's nudity. But a convent is a poor place to
seek shirt and trousers; Irwin was apologetically handed an
oversized, but dry, nun's habit which he slipped over his
head without hesitation. As a priest pointed out, "It was not

a time for jest or humor with tragedies on every side, and there was none in that vast assemblage of unfortunates who even cast a smile." Irwin plunged into the work of giving first aid to the injured, and was still dressed as a Sister of Charity when he came upon his wife, brought in from the storm by other hands.

It was before midnight when Mrs. Heideman was delivered of her child, almost immediately christened William Henry, one of four babies born that night inside convent walls.

Humor was understandably almost nonexistent, but at least one example was provided by some of the aged patients confined to the John Sealy Hospital (known affectionately as Old Red) located at the far eastern end of town, almost on the bay. One of the nurses explained: "You know we had a large number of invalids in the hospital. Many of them were very old; they were what we call confirmed invalids. I do not know that I ever knew one of them to walk a step during my two years with the hospital. They required constant care and attention. When the storm came, these lifelong invalids leaped to their feet with the agility of fifteen-year-old boys and dashed off upstairs. One of them knocked me flat on the floor in his haste to reach the second-floor landing. They walked around with sprightly gait as long as the storm lasted, but when it was over they collapsed into a helpless condition. I can't help laughing when I think about it," the nurse said, "even though they were worse off after the hurricane than they were before."

On any given day, there were seldom less than twenty large freighters berthed along Galveston's wharves, and the miscellany of smaller craft and pleasure boats gave Galveston a larger maritime population than any city along the Gulf Coast. The seamen read the storm signs earlier than any others and made their preparations accordingly. Small-craft owners removed perishables, battened hatches, secured lines, and went ashore to seek cover. There was no question of leaving the larger, two- to six-thousand-ton vessels, either from the traditional, legal, insurance or safety standpoints; and where better to ride out a storm than inside a steel hull designed to do just that?

Captain Edwin Gouge, skipper of the steamer *Kendal Castle* out of Liverpool, had streamed both anchors and a hundred feet of chain. He had seen to it that his strongest hawsers were used to secure the ship to the bollards alongside the wharf and, as an extra precaution, had ordered steel cable run out to reinforce the heavy rope that practically welded the *Kendal Castle* to its berth inside the coaling slip at the foot of 34th Street. With reason, Gouge believed that the hurricane would have to dismantle the wharf before his ship would be cast adrift in the Gulf.

On the opposite side of the slip was lashed another Britisher, the *Roma*, whose captain had the same faith in his moorings as did Gouge. When the full force of the hurricane struck the *Roma* she bucked and plunged like a mustang in a rodeo chute. Finally hawsers and cable snapped and the *Roma* was flung into the bay, propelled westward. She sheared off the ends of the new and immense Southern Pacific piers and rocketed along for nearly two miles before the random gales heeled her around and started her careening back for the wharves. She broadsided the *Kendal Castle* and nearly every other ship still tied up, then rolled up the bay to smash through the remains of the three railway bridges that connected Galveston with the mainland. The *Roma*, carrying a half-cargo and well down in the water, grounded miles away, the crewmen bruised and bleeding, but thankfully alive.

Captain Gouge felt the brutal shock when the *Roma* slammed into *Kendal Castle* and prepared for more. The steamer *Red Cross* lunged into his ship and was flung away with stove-in bows to wind up in the mud on Pelican Island across the bay. Then the little Norwegian freighter *Gyller* crashed into the *Kendal Castle*, and these blows, adding to the already terrific strain of bucking against the wind, severed the ship from its umbilicals and she started on her own wild ride up the bay. Up on the bridge, blinded by rain and hugging a stanchion, Captain Gouge had not the slightest idea where the wind was taking him; he could have been going in circles for all the good his wildly spinning compass could do him. The *Kendal Castle* finally lurched aground. Gouge had the presence of mind to order the ship's ladders dropped over the side in case there might be victims of the storm floundering around in the water. When the atmosphere cleared enough to see, Gouge looked out and saw a water tower further ashore and its familiar shape led him to believe he "was still lying near Fowler & McVitie's coal elevator." But when he gazed in another direction and saw the black-and-white striped tower of the Bolivar lighthouse off to the east he realized with a shock that he had come aground near Texas City, nearly ten miles from where the erratic voyage had begun.

Eclipsing Captain Gouge's record by far was the one set by Captain Page of the British steamer *Taunton*, which was anchored in the roads. Page put out all the anchors and kept up steam in the boilers all morning so as to be able to use his engines against the wind and the current when the hurricane got out of hand, hoping to lessen the strain on anchor chain and ship alike. This was sound seamanship, but against this hurricane there was very little even the most skillful sailor could do.

When the hard winds broke against the *Taunton,* quick reactions from the engine room to the orders from the bridge and smart handling by the helmsman enabled the ship to counter the directional force of the winds until it was almost dark. But the ship was finally overwhelmed and she pulled her anchors loose from the mud and began to move, slowly at first as the anchors dragged against the bottom, then faster as the anchor chains snapped and disappeared. The ship was shunted toward the south jetty, lofted over the top by an enormous wave, and troughed down on the other side, landing on the rocks but not holing her bottom. The *Taunton* was buffeted back and forth like a shuttlecock, driven one way by the north wind and shoved another by the mass of water rolling in from the Gulf. Captain Page, who had all but given up trying to exercise directional control, feared that sooner or later the *Taunton* would be driven up against one or the other jetty and there ground into metal mincemeat. Then the wind veered, acting in concert with the rolling tidal surge of water, and the *Taunton* was catapulted across the channel, across Pelican Spit, across the vast bowl of Galveston Bay, up what are in normal times shallow waters, and onto the mainland, where she stopped with a jolt by jamming her bows into a thirty-foot mudbank. It wasn't until the following morning that Captain Page was able to find out where they were, and when he did he was incredulous. The *Taunton,* at four thousand tons, was near a place called Cedar Point, twenty-two miles from deep water. They were, in the phraseology of that time, "in a strange land, where no ship had gone before and will probably never go again. She was in Chambers County, far out of sight of ships or city, far from the line where ships are known or where ships are seen. She was high and dry in three feet of water, there, probably, to bleach and rot." *

Over on Bolivar Peninsula, that long finger of sand pointing westward at Galveston Island, the great lighthouse on the point that was usually a lonely tomb of silence topped by a flashing brilliance was now crowded and dark, a tower of Babel for the terrified. The nine men and two women who had deserted the passenger train when it began backing up the rails on the return journey to Beaumont early that afternoon were among the first to gain admittance to the lighthouse. Before the rising wind and deepening flood made travel on the peninsula impossible, approximately 125 people had reached this beacon and were jammed inside, sitting side by side on the hard iron steps of the spiral staircase that climbed upward to the huge, and now lifeless, lens. The bottom of the tower was filled with water to a depth of several feet, and there was no way out. To those who had fled destroyed homes on desolate Bolivar the lighthouse offered the only chance for survival; but the train passengers, having exercised an option, were tortured by the thought that their chosen tower could as well be their sepulcher as their salvation.

Unlike the people in Galveston actively fighting for their

---

* A total of ten large freighters were torn from moorings and cast aground, including, *Hilarious, Benedict, Alamo, Telesfara,* and the *Norna.* Captain Gouge waited so long for the *Kendal Castle* to be dredged out and re-floated he became known as "The British Consul of Texas City." At least fifty smaller boats were tossed inland and destroyed.

lives, those trapped inside the tower could only sit. Living or dying was beyond their control. Thus immobilized, personal discomforts—real and imaginary—assume an immediate importance out of all relationship to actual need. There was no use in demanding more room from the man or woman sitting next to you, for there was none; the best that one could do to accommodate another was a shifting of a buttock, the removal of an elbow, a leaning forward. The cry went up for food, but that ended when the crowd realized none could be had. A clamor developed for water, but the small supply kept available for the lighthouse keeper was quickly exhausted by doling out to the children and a few of the women. Now that the thirst of a few had been satisfied, the craving for water became general and a few brave and reckless men risked their lives to bring relief to those parched throats.

Buckets were found and volunteers, one at a time, got outside the tower on the small observation platform and held them against the wind with both hands hoping to fill them with rain water that was pouring from the sky. The first who sampled this expensive drink spit it right out again; even though gathered from a height of 130 feet, the water was laced with brine. Many attempts were made—willingly, for it provided something to do; the action filled a real need—and finally buckets were handed down with drinkable contents.

Afterwards, when the water flowed from the base of the tower, the survivors pushed open the metal door and stepped into the dazzling sunshine. Among the flotsam surrounding the base of the tower were a dozen corpses, victims who had struggled to reach the lighthouse unseen, unheard, and much too late. Many of those among the living unashamedly dropped to their knees in the wet and evil-smelling sand and thanked God for bringing them through the worst ordeal of their lives.

Like so many others on Bolivar, Reverend L. P. Davis realized that the lighthouse would provide sanctuary for his family. Davis, who lived in a frame house on Patton Beach, did not have the benefit of Cline's warnings, and by the time he realized death was coming from the sea it was too late to reach the lighthouse, or indeed any other place. Water was pouring through the windows before Davis started to move toward his Golgotha.

Davis rushed out to the back and managed to hitch up horses to the wagon. His wife and five children waded out and scrambled aboard. Davis cracked the whip and rounded a corner of the house in time to see another wagon careen into the yard, be struck by a broadsiding wave and overturn. Davis and his two older sons jumped into the water and somehow got the passengers inside the bed of their own wagon. The rescue effort had cost long and precious minutes, and now the only place Davis could think of to go was a grove of trees about a hundred yards away. The horses struggled through the chest-high current, the wagon half-floating, half-rolling to the shelter of the trees whose leaves had been stripped away by the wind. Davis ordered his teen-age sons aloft and they lashed themselves to the trunk and branches of one of the trees with some clothesline Davis found in the wagon bed. Then he helped his wife up an adjacent tree and he followed afterward with two infants and the younger child. The neighbors imitated Davis's example; thus they were all well above the water and pinioned among the branches before the waves smashed the wagon, the wreckage dragging down the screaming horses still caught in the traces.

Blinded by the wind-whipped spray, with much of their clothing torn off, the roaring wind rendering inaudible the Reverend's shouted prayers, the treed refugees endured the hell of the hurricane, feeling the water rise up to their numbed legs before it began to fall. When the sun rose they were drained by exhaustion, their eyes red-rimmed and encrusted with salt, their skins on fire from the flaying effect of flying particles of sand; and it required great effort to disentangle themselves from the trees and reach the ground.

Davis and the others gazed upon a Sahara of desolation. Splintered wreckage lay about on the sand, scattered in pitiful piles. Davis supposed some of it belonged to him, for of his house there was no trace. Some distance away was heaped the tangle of the wagon and the drowned horses, and here and there the carcasses of farm animals were strewn. Planks, barrels and bits of furniture were washed up on the eroded beach. They shaded their eyes from the sun and peered in every direction, but there was no sign of life, no house standing, no building.

Davis got them trudging through the wet sand toward the point, but after a few minutes the women said they could not go on. The children cried with hunger and with fatigue. The others flopped down in the sand, but Davis walked on, saying he would find help. He limped on down the island, passing wreckage and occasional corpses washed ashore from Galveston, but seeing no one else. He was forced to sit down and rest several times, wondering if he and the others were the only ones left alive on the peninsula. After plodding under the fierce sun for five miles, Davis reached a farm house that had survived the storm. The owner loaned

Davis a horse and wagon and he returned for the others. They rested for two days, but saw neither salvage nor rescue parties. Food was running low, so Davis decided to lead his followers further toward the point. They kept to the beach, ruined and cluttered as it was, making poor progress because of the women and the children. They came upon a solitary steer, looking as hungry as themselves, and Davis and the other man butchered the creature to provide food.

They were near the end of their endurance when they saw a small sailboat beached high upon the dunes. She was filthy and the rigging was in shambles, but her hull was sound. Davis and the other man and the older boys managed to get the boat into the water and her bilges partially emptied. Carrying more than she was built for and with a decided list, the boat nosed slowly for Galveston.

What they would find there eclipsed anything in their previous imaginings or experience.

# Chapter 7

# NEWMAN'S TREK

INGENUITY IS SELDOM LACKING when death is moments away, and this was proved over and over again during the hours when Galveston seemed destined for extinction: the man who climbed into a stout wooden cistern and closed the lid, rolling around like a stuntman in a barrel going over Niagara Falls; the septuagenarian who saw a way to save his life by hanging on to his Newfoundland dog (appropriately named Hero) and being pulled seven blocks along Broadway until they found refuge on an elevated veranda; the horse who nosed his way inside the kitchen—and kept on going up the stairs to the second floor when the flood followed him inside the house.

A recluse living in a shanty at the far western end of the

island sat calmly in the rocking chair on his front porch watching the Gulf eat its way up the beach. He decided to stay where he was: "I was not in the center of the storm, and I had seen the water come up to my shanty many times and then recede. This time, however, the water not only came up to my little home, but into it." He waited for the water to subside, but it kept rising instead. Now alarmed, he looked around for something, anything, that would support his weight. He found a pair of large empty water jugs standing in the kitchen. He stoppered them tightly and bound them on either side of his body with rope. Cradling these improvised water wings under his arms he waded through the living room and stood on the porch. "When the crash came," he said, "I dove into the maddening waters." This part of the island was sparsely settled and there was little wreckage to contend with. He rode the Gulf like a cork in a torrent, eventually landing inland some eight miles away.

And there were a few to whom death was a matter of supreme indifference. From a second-story window of a house on 12th Street witnesses observed the familiar figure of a Negro handyman making his way through the flooded streets. He was not hurrying to high ground, but stepped inside the combined grocery store and saloon on the corner of Sealy Avenue. He stood near the window, drinking one schooner of beer after another, watching the progress of the storm outside. When the building was threatened by the rising tide and others fled the store, the beer-drinker remained where he was, helping himself to the keg. He was still standing there when the plate glass shattered and the small frame building was unhinged from its foundations and rolled down Sealy Avenue as a mass of wreckage.

John Newman was a middle-aged drought-ruined chicken farmer to whom poverty and natural disaster were cheerfully assumed as part of man's burden. Newman, who described himself as "an observer of life," was a writer of rhyming verse and had published with no spectacular success two volumes of poetry in an attempt to recoup his losses in poultry. The day of the hurricane found him employed as a casual bartender in a cheap saloon in Galveston's western end. But Newman decided to take that Saturday off; the excitement of placing himself in the heart of the city during a great storm was an irresistible lure.

Newman was abroad long before sunrise, wandering through the streets with no other purpose than absorbing the atmosphere of a town under assault and observing the behavior of its inhabitants. By noon he was unconcernedly wading along Market Street in water over his knees. He was hailed by a well-dressed fat man who asked Newman if he thought he could be ferried across the street without ruining his expensive clothes. "Sure," Newman replied. "Hand over four bits and get on my back." With the cargo astride his shoulders, Newman stepped off the curb and into the water, feeling his way carefully across the slippery wooden paving blocks. Newman, whose attention was riveted upon the difficulties of keeping his footing, was not riled when the heavy passenger "made fun of this human ass [himself] who struggled to carry this well-groomed personage to safety across the dirty waters." Newman's foot went into a deep hole where the stream had dislodged a paving block and the fat man was catapulted head first into the running water. Newman kept going, followed by threats and cursing, the half-dollar safe in his pocket.

Newman's next rescue mission came later in the afternoon with the winds building for climax, and it was much more successful. Recalled Newman, "I went along to see a German acquaintance of mine, a one-armed baker named Bush living downtown. He had recently lost his wife and was left with several small children. At Bush's request, myself and a young German took one of boys who was around seven, and between us we managed to get the boy up to City Hall, where only women and children were admitted.

"As darkness fell, I did not know what to do with myself, but by chance I found myself outside a public house. Having nowhere else to go, I went inside. I was standing in water almost up to my neck, and the barman was up on the counter serving customers with drinks. Talk about devotion to duty! Although the situation was admittedly serious, I had to laugh as I watched this man making jovial remarks as he poured out for the few customers their appointed portion of the cup that cheers." Newman downed several whiskeys, then bought a pint of brandy with the fifty cents he had earned earlier in the day, before moving through the deep water and into the uninviting darkness outside. The strong current immediately picked him up and swept him down the street.

Newman automatically began swimming, "haphazardly, not knowing nor caring where I went." Through the sound of the storm—and penetrating his own euphoria—Newman listened to a cry coming from "a fellow traveler to Eternity" somewhere out there in the darkness. At first the man pleaded for mercy and for forgiveness for his sins; then he began reviling God and all of his angels, cursing them for the calamity that was overtaking Galveston. The vileness continued until Newman heard "a cry, a yell, a gurgling sound that indicated that the merciless waters had claimed another victim."

Newman was next aware of the anguished shrilling of the sirens and whistles of the steamships in the harbor as they began breaking loose from their moorings to begin their wild flights up and down the bay. "I do not know how I managed to keep afloat," he said, "neither can I remember feeling any particular fear of death. Lethargy and spiritual apathy dominated me body and soul." Like the Negro in the grocery store, Newman felt that deliberate efforts to save one's life were ordained for failure; in the face of this cataclysm death was, sooner or later, inevitable. It was not to be welcomed as a lover, but to be accepted with resignation.

When Newman bumped against drifting lumber he instinctively embraced it, resting from the increasingly tiring effort of keeping his head above water. He took advantage of these intermissions by wrapping one arm around the timber, freeing the other hand to withdraw the brandy bottle from a trouser pocket, taking long pulls and feeling the hot liquid burn its way down to an empty stomach. To lethargy was added partial anesthesia, and he paddled numbly and unharmed through the streets, blessed with the luck God dispenses to drunks and small children, while others around him perished.

Newman had been swimming in total darkness since leaving the saloon, and when he saw a dim and yellow light in the distance he made for it. Fighting his way up the street he saw that the light came from an upstairs window in what appeared to be a boarding house, sheltered behind a large brick boot factory. Newman floated up to the second-story balcony and knocked on the sagging frame door. The yellow light moved through the house and a woman opened the door and stared at Newman, then asked what did he want? He replied somewhat ambiguously, "What do I want? What do I look like being in need of?" What Newman needed more than anything else was sleep. For thirty cents he was given a bed for the night in a windy room on a damp and salty mattress. Newman flung himself down on the bed still fully dressed in his wet and heavy clothes. Believing that if the hurricane could not kill him in the streets it was unlikely to stalk him down in that miserable room, he promptly passed out.

Sometime later—he never knew what time it was, his pocket watch having been ruined long ago—Newman was pulled partway to consciousness by the sound of monstrous kettledrums played inside his room, the shock waves reverberating through the house and rocking the foundations. Newman hazily realized that waves were battering the walls with insane fury, but the sixteen ounces of brandy and deep fatigue slid him back to oblivion.

Full consciousness returned with a terrifying crash followed by a flood of sea water that swept into the room, momentarily floating the bed. Newman sat up, wondering how many more seconds he had left to live. But the bed settled back onto the floor, the water flowed away and no other waves came. Newman rolled over and went back to sleep. "I was nothing but a spent force anyway," he said later, "and what did I care?"

When Newman awoke, sunshine was flooding the room, and he remembered feeling strangely refreshed and fiercely hungry. He got up to look for the landlady and when he went out into the hall he discovered what had caused the earsplitting crash during the night: an entire wall of the boarding house was torn away, leaving a gaping hole in the side of the building. The woman was nowhere to be found, and Newman supposed that she had been sucked into the maw of the storm when the wall was blown away.

Newman left the ruined house and wandered through the streets, now largely clear of water but deeply covered with wet sand. He plodded past tangles of telephone wires and streetcar cables, past acres of destruction, until he came upon the wreckage of a small grocery store. The sun was hot and Newman had a raging thirst. He dug into a mound of debris and uncovered an assortment of cans and bottles. Seizing a bottle of beer he broke the neck off with a tin of peas and drank it down, then another, followed by several cans of sardines washed down with more beer.

It never occurred to Newman that what he was doing was looting, that he might be shot.

# Chapter 8

# BLACK SUNDAY

**B**ECAUSE THE EYE of the hurricane moved across Galveston's latitude west of the island, the winds that swept against the town were continuous, rising and falling but never providing the half-hour or less of dead calm and the cruelly false hope that the worst is over. The winds hammered the city for fifteen hours straight before diminishing, and it wasn't until after ten that night that real abatement was noted. With the drop in wind velocity, the mass of water that had piled up on top of the island and in the bay began a sudden, disastrous outrush to the sea.

Exhausted survivors inside battered homes that had withstood the storm's greatest fury now faced a fresh and unexpected ordeal. They had seen the first, gradual rise of water sweep over the town, and when the later storm surge rolled against the walls and filled the lower floors they huddled in upstairs bedrooms and listened to the foundations crack, feeling the house shift and threaten to topple. Now, as the water level began to drop, terror subsided as well, replaced by an overwhelming sense of relief that they would live to see tomorrow, after all. Then thousands of tons of pent-up water began thundering across the island from the opposite direction, exerting inexorable ramming, then sucking, pressures that tore at buildings already weakened by the original assault. Houses were scythed down and dragged forward against earlier wreckage, killing those inside who had moments before begun to give thanks that the storm had spared them. A newspaper reporter whose own house withstood this second wave of destruction observed that the water level fell more than two and a half feet within fifteen minutes. Dr. Cline noted that there was no further damage to the town after 11 P.M., and in the thirty minutes before midnight the water dropped another four feet.

Ike Kempner, after the abortive irrigation conference in the early afternoon, had gone to his home at 16th Street and Avenue I, finding it crowded with neighbors whose prediction that Kempner's big brick house would withstand anything the hurricane could hurl at it had proved accurate. When the water began to go down, Kempner and a friend named Safford Wheeler decided to make the rounds of the neighborhood to tell everybody that the hurricane was indeed over. This was after eleven o'clock, when the great rush of water back to the sea was over and when the tide was going out at a near-normal rate. "We were cordially received in our dripping clothes," Kempner recalled, "and promptly tendered refreshments. Imbibing several at four or five residences gave us the spiritual courage to spread the good news. In high fettle we waded through knee-to-waist-deep water to downtown. We tried to gain access to the guests at the Tremont Hotel, but found the doors tightly locked and there were no answers to the doorbells or to our cries.

"So, with the wooden creosoted paving blocks we found floating in Tremont Street or resting on the sidewalks we began smashing windows to permit our philanthropic desire to advise the alarmed guests that the storm was over. We were promptly arrested by the hotel's night watchman and marched under his custody to the police station some five blocks away. We found the roof of the station building caved in, parts of which and the adjoining walls having collapsed in the streets." With no place to lodge his prisoners and with no law official present to turn them over to, the watchman had to let them go, and the happy drunks wandered back home. As they went they looked up at the dark clouds scudding across the sky and through open patches could see the stars and the moon shining brightly—but not brightly enough to illuminate the horrors that would become all too visible with the rising of the sun.

At first, none of the survivors had any clear idea of the magnitude of the disaster that had overwhelmed the city; the perspective of calamity is extremely narrow for those in its vortex. To those who had seen entire blocks of houses uprooted and cast as wreckage all over Galveston's east end, the destruction seemed complete; from the vantage point of one of the largely untouched brick mansions along Broadway, the damage appeared minimal; to one of those who survived the wiping away of every structure on the far western end of the island, all of Galveston town and its harbors and jetties and its nearly 38,000 people could have been plowed under.

Despite the frequency with which Galveston was damaged by storms, no emergency plan existed whereby the gears of city machinery would start meshing to cope with the serious problems left in the hurricane's wake. It was not until later in the day that City Hall realized just how grave these problems were, but even a cursory look outside and futile attempts to draw water from a tap and electricity from a wall plug showed that help from the mainland was needed quickly. All three bridges were down; the sewage system—old and needing replacement to begin with—was ruined; wreckage of hundreds of homes choked the downtown streets; and half-nude citizens wandered around through the slime and the sand looking for vanished and presumably dead friends and relatives.

The mayor and a dozen or so of Galveston's more energetic businessmen gathered in one of the downtown office buildings still standing and decided to send word to Houston by the only means available, across the bay by boat if one could be found seaworthy enough to negotiate the still-rough waters. W. L. Moody, Jr., volunteered the use of his father's steam yacht, *Pherabe*, a twenty-footer with shallow draft. A contractor with experience at sea named Lawrence Elder volunteered to act as captain, and two brokers, a railroad engineer and a pair of newspaper reporters offered to act as crew and messengers to the outside world.

Just before the *Pherabe* cast off from the ruined pier, Father Kirwin rushed up and spoke to Richard Spillane, the commercial editor of the Galveston *Tribune*. He had just walked through his parish, which extended cross-city, and was "impressed with the damage." He said that he had not yet seen the eastern beach area, nor had he had time to look at the far western end, but from what he had seen he believed that the loss of life was not as great as one would imagine. He told Spillane, "Don't exaggerate. It is better that we underestimate the loss of life than we put the figure too high and find it necessary to reduce it later. If I were in your place," said the cleric, "I don't believe I would put the loss of life at more than five hundred."

The *Pherabe* got underway at 11 A.M. and almost immediately ran into trouble. The short bow banged into the troughs of the waves that serrated the bay and Elder had difficulty in getting the boat to answer to the helm. Water crashed over the side and the crew were kept busy bailing, some of them getting dangerously near to seasickness, a condition not alleviated by the sight of swollen corpses bobbing up and down among the flotsam. Elder manhandled the small yacht to Texas City, eight miles away, and there too they saw wreckage. Elder thought it was hopeless to try to get the inadequate boat all the way to Houston, so they tied up at Texas City and rented a wagon that took them three miles to La Marque, the nearest rail station. Nobody could tell them when the next train was due, but one of them saw a handcar sitting on a siding, so they all got aboard and started pumping their way north.

Poor Spillane. His feet were on fire with pain. The exertions, the rising heat and humidity, the salt-water soaking, and the ordeal of nerves during the past twenty-four hours brought on a violent attack of eczema and he was almost mad with itching and soreness. Fifteen miles up the track they saw a train bearing down on them from League City. They stopped the tiresome handcar and flagged down the train. They explained their urgent mission to the conductor, who obstinately refused to back up and take them to Houston. His destination, he said, was La Marque and that was where he was going. Fuming, the crew of the *Pherabe* got aboard after ditching the handcar, and traveled back along the same track they had just worked so hard to traverse. The wind had blown down the lines in a wide swath, so there was nothing the messengers could accomplish in the dreary little town. The railroad track was ripped up south of there, and the entire afternoon was wasted while the conductor immobilized the train, unable to make a decision. Finally, around midnight, he decided under pressure that he might as well return to Houston. Spillane and the others arrived there to find the town dark, but the telegraph lines were still up. Spillane had to be carried into the telegraph office, where he got off duplicate wires to President William McKinley and Texas Governor Joseph D. Sayers.

Spillane, remembering Father Kirwin's words about using restraint and yet wanting to impress upon the Federal and State authorities the urgent need for help, sent off the following message, dated September 10.

> I have been deputized by the mayor and the Citizens' Committee of Galveston to inform you that the city of Galveston is in ruins, and certainly many hundreds, if not a thousand, are dead. The tragedy is one of the most frightful in recent time. Help must be given by the state and nation or the suffering will be appalling. Food, clothing and money will be needed at once. The whole south side of the city for three blocks in from the gulf is swept clear of every building, the whole wharf front is a wreck and but few of the houses in the city are really habitable. The water supply is cut off and the food stock damaged by salt water. All bridges

are washed away and stranded steamers litter the bay. When I left this morning the search for bodies had begun. Corpses were everywhere. Tempest blew eighty-four miles an hour and then carried government instruments away. At same time waters of gulf were over whole city, having risen twelve feet. Water has now subsided and the survivors are left helpless among the wreckage, cut off from the world except by boat.

RICHARD SPILLANE

Spillane, his primary mission accomplished, allowed himself to be carried off to a doctor to have his feet looked after, not knowing that it would be a week before he would be able to get back to Galveston and not knowing that his estimate of the situation there was woefully understated. In view of what other journalists would report, this was something Spillane could later well be proud of.

On the same train that perversely brought Spillane and the others back to La Marque was a compositor from the Houston *Post* named W. L. Love, whose wife and son were in Galveston for the weekend. Love was frantic for news of his family, and unable to get through to Galveston by telephone he determined to get there by any means he could. From La Marque he walked to Texas City, but could not find anybody willing to row him across the bay. Love saw a cypress railway tie lying on the shore and it gave him an idea. He located a coal shovel from the cab of a derelict locomotive engine and went back to the tie and shoved it into the water. Using the heavy shovel as an oar, Love started paddling for the island which he could see through the haze. The bay had calmed somewhat during the early afternoon, and by keeping his legs straddled over the heavy tie and into the water Love managed to keep aboard during the six hard hours of paddling it took him to reach Galveston. He was among the first from the mainland to reach the battered city, and what he encountered during the hours of traipsing through the streets to find his wife and child appalled him.

The eastern section of town was scythed clean of frame houses, leaving only piles of loose planking as far as his eye could see looking down the beach. How many blocks were gone? A hundred? Two hundred? Love couldn't guess. He stumbled over broken furniture, pots, pans, and unrecognizable bits of household goods scattered everywhere, half-buried in the sand. When he passed the big piles of wreckage, where one or more houses had been telescoped, he saw people pulling at the boards and knew they were looking for the dead buried deep underneath the tons of wood. And there were dead sprawled everywhere; a body spread in a pool of water with sightless eyes staring at the sky, nude and crucified; one resting on a pile of lumber, draped by some passer-by; four or five lying drowned and crushed underneath a collapsed corner of a house—the whole family, probably.

The familiar beach was littered with them, intermingled with the carcasses of livestock and household pets, rocking back and forth in the warm salt water at the edge of the beach. The once-smooth shoreline was now ragged and torn—and began far inland, washing into the ruins of front yards that had been many hundred feet from the water before the hurricane.

The great warehouses along the wharves were mostly smashed in on one side, unroofed and shattered throughout their length. The contents were either piled in heaps along the wharves or scattered in the streets. Small tugs and sail-boats were jammed halfway inside buildings along the bay, flung there by incoming waves and left there by the receding water. In the rail yards behind the wharves hundreds of heavy box cars were jumbled in disorderly piles, filled with hundreds of thousands of dollars' worth of flour, grain, cotton and cottonseed. Miles of track were uprooted and buried in sand. The massive derailment continued for more than two miles, passing a few feet from one of the only small buildings still standing, an eight-windowed structure housing the Deep Water Saloon.

The heart of the business district was a shambles. Fallen telephone poles and tangled wires and ruined buggies and piles of brick and even the wreckage of houses filled the streets, making passage almost impossible. Already the place was beginning to smell horribly, at first from the tons of vegetables that had been washed into the streets when the doors of the big warehouses were smashed open. Now these vegetables were piled in the streets in mounds of rotting garbage.

It wasn't until two that afternoon that Mayor Walter C. Jones, a bald, heavy-moustached, and inoffensive-looking man, was able to convene an *ad hoc* committee charged with keeping Galveston, then a derelict ship lying foul and dead in the water, from sliding into anarchy and becoming a pestilential sandspit breeding further deaths from disease. The Committee of Public Safety, as it was called, was headed by a railway executive named J. H. Hawley, whose own house had suffered little damage and whose family was safely out of town when the hurricane struck.

Hawley's two operational deputies were Ed Ketchum,

Two weeks after hurricane once-proud streets still resembled
battlefields. Myriad tracks trace paths of wagons shoving aside debris
in search for the dead. This horse, one of few animals left alive,
stands morosely in wreckage of Avenue M. *(The Rosenberg Library)*

Homes. Wind and water and jagged timbers broke backs of
strongest structures . . .

. . . turned them upside down. Searchers could only ask, Whose trunk? Whose body? *(The Rosenberg Library)*

Duplex homes were split apart, others were moved off foundations
and tipped askew. Owners rummaged in fetid pools seeking some
treasured object, some souvenir of those swallowed by the storm.
The house above, no stronger than its neighbors, miraculously
remained upright among splintered remains of homes flung from
blocks around. The civilian militia has already begun to arm.
(*The Rosenberg Library*)

Ordeal of uncovering and carrying the dead began even before
water had subsided from downtown streets. They were everywhere.
The man at right succeeded in identifying wife by earrings she wore
on that fateful Saturday night. Thousands simply vanished.
(*The Rosenberg Library*)

Expedient of sending the dead to sea aboard vile barges was abandoned when the press was too great, when the sea returned its burdens to the stricken town. Then the order went out to burn the hurricane's victims where they lay, singly and in droves. Illustrator who was not there conjured fanciful scene of multi-racial looters defiling the fair white dead. Ships were hurled from accustomed moorings, stranded miles away in mud. (*The Rosenberg Library*)

Exodus to the mainland began when storm had passed. Thousands
perished, more hundreds gathered up what was left to patch together
another life in another place. But most remained, convinced that
life could never again deal them a worse blow. This couple, dressed
in their Sunday best, walk to church through phoenix ruins.
(*The Rosenberg Library*)

Galveston's tough Chief of Police, and an Ohioan recently arrived in Galveston named L. R. D. Fayling who, after a checkered career, was in Galveston managing a national newspaper syndicate. Fayling had learned to deal with unruly crowds six years earlier as a deputy U.S. Marshal during the bloody Chicago strikes. For a time he had been an undercover agent, as he described himself, in the Appalachian states dueling with moonshiners. In 1895 he went to Cuba seeking adventure and found it working for the Junta, both as spy and as a captain operating in the hills with Cuban guerrillas. Captured by the Spanish, Fayling spent time in sordid jails, but managed to escape with his life if not his health. In 1898, Fayling raised a company of volunteers to return to Cuba to deal with his old enemies during the Spanish-American War.

Fayling, who had spent all night in the business district helping in the rescue of those floundering in the water, turned up at the wrecked City Hall not long after the sun came up, looking for Chief Ketchum. He was told to try the Tremont Hotel, the temporary headquarters for the city's administration. Fayling, still wearing his long woolen bathing suit and what were described as "a pair of stout Turkish slippers," found Ketchum and the Mayor and volunteered his services. He had, he said, seen people crawling inside buildings and stores, apparently bent on looting whatever was available, If, as he suspected, not enough of Galveston's seventy policemen were left alive or fit to maintain order, could he raise a volunteer force to maintain law and order in the city? Fayling's offer was seized upon, and he was asked to come back at two that afternoon to get his credentials. Fayling returned to his house and changed into his Ohio militia uniform—short blue jacket, white duck pants, belt, and cap—picked up his .30-30 Winchester that had last seen action in West Virginia, and went back to the Tremont. Hawley wrote out Fayling's orders on hotel stationery, promoting him to major on the spot.

Fayling was named "Commander in Chief of the military forces and special deputies of the Police . . . only subject to the orders of the undersigned, the Mayor and the Chief of Police." The paper was countersigned by Chief Ketchum, who added that the major was authorized to requisition any property he might require for the use of his force, his receipt honored and such property paid for by the City of Galveston. Thus armed, Fayling went out in the streets to find his men. First thing you do, Ketchum told him, is close down every last saloon in town.

Hawley estimated that there were anywhere from eight to ten thousand homeless people wandering the streets of Galveston, and these would have to be somehow fed and sheltered. The dead? Probably more than a thousand, now that he had had the time to get a better look at the devastation. Once Fayling got his militia organized, it would be a relatively simple matter to round up and guard the undamaged food supplies on the island, but the question of water was a far more serious one; the pumping station was wrecked and the clear artesian water flowing through a thirty-six-inch pipe under the bay from wells eighteen miles away could not be drawn. The one encouraging factor was that there were so few critically injured to care for and that the hospitals, save for plumbing and electricity, were in good shape and would be able to handle the load. The explanation for the small numbers of injured requiring hospitalization is that the overwhelming number of deaths resulted from drowning, where there are no halfway markers separating life from death. And to be injured by flying debris meant usually to be knocked into the current, or weakened to the point where it was no longer possible to retain a grip on floating timbers, or on roofs, which meant falling into the maelstrom and drowning before shock or loss of blood could stop the heartbeat.

With Spillane and the others on the way to Houston to return, hopefully, with massive quantities of food, water and medical supplies, with Fayling out rounding up supernumerary policemen, Hawley's main concern was with the dead, and to these he now turned.

# Chapter 9

# THE CITY SCOURGED

**M**ULE-DRAWN DRAYS that had been used on Saturday morning to deliver groceries, beer or bags of grain were filled that long Sunday afternoon with corpses, piled four and five deep, and wheeled through the streets to a makeshift morgue near the docks. At first, the bodies were handled with reverence; the volunteer workers realizing that the loads they lifted from the wagons were, after all, fathers, mothers, sons and daughters only yesterday, and they were laid gently in neat rows on the damp concrete flooring of the big shed chosen to house the remains. Bodies that were still clothed were searched for papers that would prove identity; those who were nude were examined for tattoos or jewelry that might contain clues. Afterwards the

bodies were covered with tarpaulin, cotton sacking, and anything else at hand, and numbered pieces of paper were laid
on the upper halves, the numbers recorded in a warehouse
ledger book against whatever information could be gleaned
from the grisly search procedures.

These wagons of the dead crawled through the torpid
city hour after hour, the work becoming increasingly unpleasant as the sun climbed higher in the brassy sky. At
10 A.M. the temperature was already at 85 degrees, and at
six that afternoon stood at eighty-eight. Before dark there
were more than five hundred corpses ranked inside the
morgue, and the sun beating against the crumpled corru-
gated roof turned the place into an oven. Carrion bluebot-
tle flies swarmed, the insistent droning magnified by the
amphitheater-like acoustics of the hollow shed. Into this
charnel house streamed survivors, fearfully lifting the coverings, going away sadly or collapsing with the shock of final-
ity, depending upon what they found. Among them was
Hawley, who would later write his wife:

"I lifted a pall and found beneath it, with a faint smile on
her lips, Mrs. Wakelee, with her grey hair all matted and
streaming in disordered confusion about her shoulders. I
next lifted the pall of Walter Fisher, the husband of Lillie
Harris, and then came to Richard Swain, whom you no
doubt remember. . . . Lillie Harris Fisher and all her children are dead; also Mrs. Rebecca Harris and three of the
Davenport children, but one of them was saved. Davenport
laid his hand in mine and said, Mr. Hawley, we know you
mourn with us. I am grateful to God for at least saving our
little daughter."

Many bodies were found in the desolation of the western
beaches, and attempts were made to bury them on the spot;

but after two or three shovelfuls of earth were turned the blades slid into watery sand and the project was abandoned. The Galveston cemetery, so derided by the British diplomat Sheridan, many years before, was itself a ruin; coffins and bones were mixed in among tumbled crosses and headstones in a macabre compost of ancient remains and faded memories; the graves were filled with sea water and the whole was overlaid with slime and debris. By Sunday night, with bodies still arriving in the rapidly filling morgue by the drayful, Hawley realized that any hope of orthodox burial was futile.

Early Monday morning, Hawley called the members of the Committee of Public Safety together and told them that the existence of Galveston's living depended upon how rapidly the town could get rid of its dead; the Christian reverence for escorting the departed to the promised land with solemnity, sermons, black crape and organ music would have to be ruthlessly done away with. A man named Morrissey spoke up, saying that since the sea had killed them, let the sea receive its victims. Undamaged barges were tied up in the slips not far from the morgue, and Hawley ordered the corpses hauled aboard.

The work, which the day before had been heartbreaking and repugnant, now became nauseating. The dreadful loads had lost the convenient stiffness that facilitated handling and had become grotesquely swollen, soft masses giving off odors that seared the nostrils and triggered gag reflexes. Ed Ketchum sent for a cask of whiskey and any strong cigars that could be found. The workers were doled out walloping amounts of bourbon, told to light up the stogies, and informed that alcohol-soaked handkerchiefs made effective masks against the smell of death.* Thus fortified, the handlers continued with the gruesome task. The bodies were piled on anyhow, some flopping face down, some face up, many of them nude, and all of them hated burdens to those who flung them onto the hard wooden decking, oblivious to the wet, heavy sounds they made when they landed. There was neither material at hand nor time to find coverings for the dead; they went to sea as graceless as mute and derelict tramps.

The first bargeload was towed into the Gulf at noon, and it was discovered that there were not enough heavy weights aboard to go around for the four hundred or so bodies to be consigned to the deep. Thus many went over the side two and three together, and some had to be dropped overboard as they were. It was done with compelling haste, and with no more ceremony than would be shown in disposing of thirty tons of garbage.

Clarence Ousley, Editor of the Galveston *Tribune,* observed that "Human nature has its limitations. The men in the morgues and at the wharf sickened and recoiled. Fresh recruits were brought in, some volunteers, some impressed at the point of the bayonet. One rebelled and tried to incite his fellows to resistance. He was felled like an ox and tumbled onto the barge." The "volunteers" were told that if the corpses were not removed by sundown they could not be removed at all except in fragments, and doctors warned that if the morgues were not cleared by the next morning the buildings would have to be zoned off and burned to the

---

* A procedure familiar to the rubber-gloved and booted members of American Graves Registration Unit members forty-five years later when searching for battlefield dead in France and Germany during and after World War II.

ground. The frantic loading went on, and late that afternoon Hawley could record that more than seven hundred
bodies had been thrown into the sea. Many of them were
washed back ashore with the incoming tide.

Major Fayling lost little time in rounding up a force of
vigilantes to police the town. Recruits were gathered from
the local militia, Galveston's own Sharpshooters, leavened
with a handful of ragged artillerymen, and joined by what
were described as responsible citizens, men who either had
a real desire to protect property or to whom the novelty of
carrying a gun in the streets was an irresistible lure. This
motley force, when added to by about sixty of the city's
surviving regular police officers, totaled approximately three
hundred men. They were variously uniformed and randomly
armed. The militiamen's colorful uniforms, dating back to
the styles popular during and after the Civil War, clashed
with the more functional dark blue caps of the artillery
regulars, most of whom could only find bits and pieces of
uniform to begin with because everything they owned had
been swept away with the collapse of the barrack; some had
jackets, but no regulation trousers; some had leggins but no
shoes; some had shoes but no socks. There were not enough
of the big .30-40 Krag-Jorgensen rifles—the kind used a short
time before to civilize the Moros in the Philippines—to go
around, so Fayling used the carte-blanche given him by the
Committee and appropriated Winchesters and six-shooters
from retail merchants. Fayling himself commandeered a
horse wandering loose in the streets and told all those who
considered themselves good horsemen to do the same; with
nearly ten square miles to patrol, Fayling wanted a cavalry
arm.

Galveston was like the carcass of a fresh-killed steer, supine, partially open, offering rich pickings to scavengers. Looting, once started, is a virulent disease, and Fayling was told to deal with it in summary fashion.

What happened during the next twenty-four hours between Fayling's men and those who prowled the streets seeking plunder was never fully documented. But the reports that emerged from the city during the week following the hurricane were nothing short of sensational, and if these reports are worthless as facts they at least serve the purpose of revealing contemporary attitudes, and provide clues as to what the general population of the country was prepared to accept as truth.

What *is* known is that Fayling's men patrolled the smashed town on foot and on horseback for nearly thirty-six hours without relief, that householders sitting in the darkness said they "felt a great sense of security" because of the presence of some kind of law in the city, that there were instances of household and mercantile robbery and plundering of the dead, and that there was gunfire that resulted in the killing of a handful of looters. Probably the closest to the truth can be found in the following item that appeared in the Galveston *News* on Thursday, September 13. The staid *News* thought so little of what had happened that the story was buried on the fifth page, and ran:

### WORK OF THE POLICE
*Seven Negroes Killed*
*Who Were Detected*
*Robbing the Dead*

GALVESTON, *Tuesday*—Orders were issued to soldiers and police to kill any person caught in the act of robbing the dead. Up to Tuesday morning seven negroes were caught robbing the dead and paid the penalty with their lives. They were shot dead and their bodies carted away with the victims of the storm.

There may have been more depredations and killings by the army of guards scattered about the city, but these seven cases have been verified by *News* reporters although there is no detailed record at police headquarters. . . .

One of the few to give his name as witness to a street execution was J. C. Roberts, who arrived in Galveston from Houston on Monday seeking information about his employer's relatives. Roberts's first move was to enter a drugstore and ask for whiskey because he was "worn out." He was refused, but a doctor told him he would be happy to write out a prescription for $5, or about five times the usual price. The druggist then sold Roberts a small bottle of bourbon for $2.50, using the doctor's yardstick as a mark-up guide. Roberts went outside, and along 20th Street, "saw dead everywhere. They were scattered on every hand and nearly all in a complete state of nudity. He saw an Italian woman standing in the street holding in her hand the foot and leg of an infant severed from the little body. She was unclad, but alive and insane, and refused to leave the pile of debris which contained the remains of her little one."

Walking on, Roberts "witnessed one of the guards shoot five Negro looters. He had observed one of them men robbing a dead body. The man refused to desist and the guard shot him dead as he kneeled on the ground. Four companions of the ghoul started to assault the guard, who threw himself on his stomach and, firing rapidly, killed them all."

In Chicago, a summer visitor to Galveston who had sur-

vived the storm to return home to Illinois was interviewed
by reporters eager for first-hand information. Alice Pixley
told how she and her friend, Lulu George, fled the George
home on 35th Street to seek shelter inside a two-story building, where mounting terror and the sight of "crushed and
mangled bodies whirling past in a jumble of timbers and
debris, . . . men, women and children sinking, floating,
dashing on I knew not where" caused her to faint, awaken-
ing with Lulu George's cry, *"Alice, we are saved!"* ringing
in her ears.

"The day we left," said Miss Pixley, "the militia was out
in all its force. I could hear the sharp reports of a rifle and
the wail of some soul as he paid the penalty for his thieving
operations. Later I saw the soldiers with their glistening
rifles leveled at scores of men and saw them topple forward
dead. Oh, they had to shoot those terrible beasts, for they
were robbing the dead. They groveled in blood, it seems. I
saw with my own eyes the fingers of women cut off by
regular demons in search for jewels. The soldiers came and
killed them and it was well."

Did Alice Pixley see these things? Did she actually say
she saw them? She was so quoted in the Chicago dailies,
her story later reprinted in at least one book that appeared
in an astonishingly short time after the hurricane.

Young Alexander Spencer—son of Stanley G. Spencer,
who was killed on Saturday morning while sitting in Ritter's
Cafe and Saloon—survived the storm, along with his mother,
brother, five grown dogs, three puppies and three black cats,
in one of three houses left standing in their neighborhood.
Pressed for details, Spencer said, "We did not see any of
the Negroes stealing, as mother kept us in the house all

the time, but we could hear the shots. They commenced this dastardly work Sunday night. The ghouls are composed of foreigners and Negroes."

The New York *Journal*, aware of the limitless human-interest potential inside the wrecked city, dispatched one of the paper's leading feature writers, a woman named Winifred Black, to Galveston by the earliest train. At Texas City, where the train stopped, Miss Black "begged, cajoled and cried my way through the line of soldiers with drawn swords who guard the wharf, and sailed across the bay on a little boat which is making irregular trips to meet the relief trains from Houston."

The trip across the bay was made at night, and Miss Black struck up a conversation with one of the federal marshals who "took off his broad hat and let the starlight shine on his strong face." When the boat reached Galveston harbor Miss Black gagged at the smell that hung over the town, and when she stepped ashore she was challenged by an armed sentry. The marshal got her through the picket line, and together they walked through the blacked-out streets. Miss Black queried the lawman about the guards and the work they did.

"The best men!" said the marshal. "They've left their own misery and come down here to do police duty. We needed them. They had to shoot twenty-five men yesterday for looting the dead. Not Americans," the marshal assured her, "not one of them. I saw them all—Negroes and the poor whites from southern Europe. They cut off the hands of their victims."

Winifred Black secured a room at the Tremont Hotel, and the following morning she was abroad gathering material. "I came upon a group of people in a bystreet," she wrote, "a man and two women, all colored. The man was big and muscular. One of the women was old and one was young. They were digging in a heap of rubbish, and when they heard my footsteps the man turned an evil, glowering face upon me and the young woman hid something in the folds of her dress. Human ghouls, these, prowling in search of prey. A moment later there was noise and excitement in the little narrow street, and I looked back and saw the Negro running with a crowd at his heels. The crowd caught him and would have killed him, but a policeman came up. They tied his hands and took him through the streets with a whooping rabble at his heels. It goes hard with a man in Galveston caught looting these days.

"A young man well known in the city shot and killed a Negro who was cutting the ears from a dead woman's head to get her earrings out. The Negro lay in the street like a dead dog, and not even the members of his own race would give him the tribute of a kindly look." So reported Miss Black.

As thin and suspicious as these first-person accounts may be, they are marvels of solid documentary journalism when compared with the flood of unsigned articles that appeared even while Galveston's wreckage was being cleared away. Fayling was a natural focus for attention, and was credited with wholesale destruction of miscreants. "Tuesday night," one story began, "ninety Negro looters were shot in their tracks by citizen guards. One of them was searched and $700 found, together with four diamond rings and two water-soaked gold watches. The finger of a white woman with a gold band around it was clutched in his hands.

"In the afternoon a mounted squad was detailed by Major Fayling to search a house where Negro looters were known to have secreted plunder. 'Shoot them in their tracks, boys! We want no prisoners,' said the Major. At six o'clock, a report reached Major Fayling that twenty Negroes were robbing a house at 19th and Beach Streets. 'Plant them!' commanded the young Major, as a half-dozen citizen soldiers, led by a corporal, mustered before him for orders. 'I want everyone of those twenty Negroes dead or alive,' said the Major.

"The squad left on the double quick. Half an hour later they reported ten of the plunderers killed."

Accounts gathered by Murat Halstead, author and journalist in faraway Chicago, included scenes of pitched battles. "A horde of Negro rowdies attacked a squad of soldiers guarding St. Mary's Hospital Monday night. Hundreds of shots were fired and sixteen Negroes were killed." Four paragraphs later, the battle was moved up to Sunday night, the horde of Negroes were all armed this time, and Sergeant Camp was credited with four kills, sharing his triumph with the rest of the squad who bagged another dozen.

Pockets "bulged with fingers," and even ears; the record was twenty-three fingers in one pocket, which must have been of enormous size. "Bullet-riddled bodies dangled from lamp posts" all over Galveston. Fayling was shown to play no favorites when it was described how his vigilantes left behind on Avenue P a windrow of both white and black "fiends" who were lined up on the curb and mercilessly gunned down. A Negro caught cutting the ring finger from a young (white) girl was "pumped full of Winchester bullets." Negroes in platoon-strength "hordes" of fifty caught rifling corpses enmeshed in the ruins of an apartment house were arrested and lined up against a brick wall and slaughtered. Faulty aim was put right by a sergeant delivering the *coup de grâce* with a pistol. White women were robbed and raped in broad daylight, sometimes individually and sometimes by hordes. "Thieves and Vampires" were buttressed by desperadoes making their way to the stricken island from as far away as Austin and New Orleans in order to share in the plunder and the fun.

It is thanks to a Pullman porter named Michael B. Hancock, who lived on Dearborn Street in Chicago, that Latin-Americans were spared the ignominy of being left unmentioned in the chronicle of those first few days after the storm. Hancock and his conductor, Frank Alphons, decided to join a relief train running out of Austin to Texas City. After difficulties in getting across the bay and through the picket lines, Hancock and Alphons at last reached Galveston. They were immediately impressed by the militia to help in gathering the dead; this was not at all what they had in mind when they left Austin, but neither wanted to quarrel with an armed militiaman and they "feigned acquiescence." While waiting to be told what to do, Hancock and his conductor watched another group under guard lassoing bodies piled on top of wreckage and dragging them to the ground.

Recalled Hancock: "A terrible outcry arose from the men engaged in this work. Running quickly to the scene of the trouble we saw one of the workers was in the grasp of one of the soldiers. The man, a Mexican in shabby clothes and wearing a drooping sombrero, was standing sullenly eyeing the crowd with one hand in his pocket. The hand was dragged from his pocket and five mutilated fingers dropped to the ground. Each finger had one or more rings on it. The other workers seemed to go mad, and with cries of 'Lynch him! Burn him!' made for the unfortunate wretch."

Hancock described how the intervention of soldiers saved

the Mexican from mob violence in time to be shot to death moments later by a firing squad from a distance of ten feet. The work of recovering bodies resumed, but it was not for Hancock. "I told Alphons that I never could stand the notion of handling bodies. He agreed with me, and we edged away from the soldiers and made a run for the beach, where we hired a small boy to row us to the mainland. It will be a long time before I want to go back to Galveston," he concluded.

A perceptive editor in Baltimore, Nathan Green, in going over endless accounts concerning what is supposed to have happened between the militia and the looters observed, "There are no official records; it was not intended that there should be any. If there was shooting, the criminal should be buried where he was killed. But these stories grew after they left Galveston, and when they were repeated several times between the island and Houston they were much magnified. The looters summarily dealt with," concluded Green, "increased in numbers like Falstaff's men in buckram." *

To Captain Evans, standing on the bridge of the *Comal*, steering her through the littered Gulf with the island clearly in view, it seemed that Galveston was on fire; palls of greasy black smoke hung over the town, unmoving in the humid air. Evans and his crew had fought their ship through the

---

* See *Henry IV*, Part I, Act II, Scene 4, where Falstaff's enemies magically increase in number during Falstaff's ever-changing account of his fight in the woods with men dressed in rough forest garb. Adding the totals from the various accounts would indicate that there were more blacks and "foreigners" killed during a forty-eight hour period than soldiers died inside the Alamo during the thirteen-day siege. Fayling left no tally sheet, but in a letter to her parents in Chicago a secretary at Clarke & Courts Stationers, Nellie Cary, wrote: "Major Fayling, at our house, is in command of the protective force. They have had to shoot many to keep the horrible ghouls under control." Fayling did not tell Miss Cary just what "many" might signify.

hurricane after leaving Key West five days earlier, and they had no idea what to expect when they reached home port. Extensive wind and water damage could reasonably be assumed, but the idea of a conflagration remained puzzling and alien until the ship was tied up in the clutter of the Mallory Line wharf (less damaged than any of the others), where Evans and the crew learned what their nostrils had already suggested: the smoke was rising from pyres, and it was not the city that was roasting, but human flesh.

The burning began at sunrise on Tuesday morning following a disheartening meeting between the members of the Public Safety Committee and the medical staff of the John Sealy Hospital. The doctors warned that if radical measures were not taken to dispose of Galveston's dead, and taken immediately, they could not guarantee against the outbreak of a plague that would kill off more people by disease than were done in by the hurricane. Corpses were scattered all over the island, and it was feared that the number buried under the mounds of wreckage on the east end would run into the thousands. There was no time, the doctors said, to use yesterday's method of disposal by barging the dead out to sea; too many of them were returning, and they did not want drayloads of purulence being hauled through the streets to the wharves.

At first, long trenches were dug and filled with alternate layers of scrap lumber and the dead. Masked men carrying cans of fuel oil sloshed the volatile liquid the length of the trench and carefully applied a torch. Flames whooshed up satisfactorily and the slow burning process began. To speed things up, the workers ceased digging trenches and instead combed bodies from areas two blocks square and dragged them to a central collecting point where they were burned among piles of loose wreckage. As many as a dozen of these pyres would be burning at a time at different places within the city, and Galveston's firemen were kept busy hopping from one place to another to see to it that the fires did not spread. Most of their pumpers were wrecked, and with no pressure in the mains a conflagration, once started, could not be stopped, and the entire city would be incinerated.

In the brutal heatwave that smothered the city, the rate of decomposition was rapid; the bodies were simply falling apart when they were lifted or shoveled onto the carts for transfer to the collecting points. In some instances Fayling's bayonets were needed to keep the workers on the job. In desperation the superintendents of the work gangs pleaded to be allowed to torch wreckage wherever it was found, consuming everything within and thus obviating the necessity of separating fragments of flesh and carting them away under the merciless sun. The *News* warned against this in an editorial.

"Once let the fire demon get hold of the immense masses of lumber and the remaining portion of the city may be wiped out. Many partially wrecked houses are in the piles and household goods belonging to people who have lost everything may be recovered." The editor pointed out that it was folly to burn hundreds of thousands of running feet of lumber; it would be needed to provide temporary shelter for the city's thousands of homeless. "These people must be cared for. Some are now crowded in the homes of friends while others are located in the large buildings in the business district, and there is no reason why the wreckage should not be used for the temporary sheltering of the homeless without regard for the fire rules of the city as they now stand. Lumber promises to be a scarce article once the resumption of building is begun, and every board, rafter and scantling in the piles of wreckage should be saved." To some extent, this was done, but when—as happened more than once—a disposal squad faced a small mountain of wreckage made up of four or five splintered homes all jammed together, where the stench seeping up through the twisted planks indicated perhaps thirty or forty corpses were rotting inside, the great pile was put to the torch and nobody blamed them.

At the end of the first day of burning, crews reported that about a thousand bodies, give or take a hundred or so, had been gathered and cremated. The fires burned through the night, and people on the mainland stood on their own maimed and darkened shore to watch the island glowing dully orange on the horizon. Fayling and his men gave thanks for the fires that lighted the ruins, for it enabled them to detect, pursue and (as we have noted) execute scavengers of the dead.

On Tuesday morning Mayor Jones learned from Ed Ketchum and Fayling the extent of the previous day's repression of looters, and was disturbed at the report by one of Fayling's men that he had been fired upon by a man carrying a revolver, probably stolen, but whose aim was not as deadly as the trooper's. Jones dictated an eighty-five-word flyer placing Galveston under martial law, forbidding citizens to carry guns except by written permission and ordering all arms and ammunition to be turned over to Fayling. The order was hurriedly printed and posted all over town. He next turned his attention to attempts at looting the living. Explained a penmanship teacher from Dallas named G. W. Ware, "The mercenary commercial pirates began a harvest of extortion. The price of bacon was pushed up to fifty cents a pound, bread to sixty cents a loaf, and owners of small schooners and other sailing craft formed a trust and charged eight dollars a passenger for transportation across the bay to the mainland.

"Mayor Jones and other men of conscience were shocked at these proceedings, and the Mayor decided to confiscate all foodstuffs and other necessities for the common good. Bread came down to ten cents a loaf, bacon dropped to fifteen cents a pound and the price for a voyage across the bay was set at $1.50 a passenger. Accounts are being kept of all sales of foodstuffs and settlements will be made at scheduled rates."

Jones divided the city into twelve wards, appointing a well-known and usually respected Galveston businessman as chairman of each ward. "Your first duty," he said, "is to provide a central store or house as near to your ward as can be reached by dray. Order by drayload from any wholesale grocery [the required] staples. It is your duty to have assistants who, together with yourself, will remain from 7 A.M. to 6 P.M. and supply all the people in your ward direct. It is your duty to organize a working force and clean up the debris in your ward in such manner as you deem best." Then the mayor made one point unmistakably clear: "Any ablebodied man," he concluded, "who will not volunteer for this work must not be fed."

The mayor was making all the right moves, but massive help was needed from outside to scour Galveston, to feed its hungry, to quench the thirst of its people, to shelter its homeless thousands, to aid the sick, to finish getting rid of its dead.

The first help trickled in that morning. The steamer *Law-*

*rence* pulled in from Houston carrying several tons of provisions and four huge tanks of fresh water, 100,000 gallons in all. And at six that evening a yawl tied up at the ruined wharf and discharged Brigadier General Thomas Scurry, adjutant general of the Texas State Volunteer Guard, and his staff. Scurry, a tall, lean man with a small head, large eyes and flowing moustache, went immediately to the Tremont and set up a headquarters, then closeted himself with the key members of the Committee and began asking salient questions pertaining to Galveston's survival and resurrection. Within forty-eight hours, Scurry had landed more than two hundred well-armed and smartly uniformed state militiamen, and trains from San Antonio and St. Louis were bringing fifty thousand individual rations and a thousand army tents to be used to keep the refugees out of the elements. Mayor Jones proclaimed martial law for the second time, named General Scurry as the new commandant of the provisional forces, and Scurry, who found increasing resistance among workers to handle the dead, issued General Order Number Nine.

Scurry ordered guards and gang foremen to exercise "due diligence toward preventing hardships on private individuals, or impressing for service. However," he pointed out, "individual interests must give way to the general good . . . procrastination will bring pestilence to finish the dire work of the hurricane. . . . The interests of no individual, firm or corporation will for one instant be spared to secure volunteers for work." *

As it turned out, Scurry's diligent men made far fewer

---

* Among the units serving under Scurry were the Houston Light Guards, the Trezevant Rifles, the Forth Worth Fencibles, the Dallas Rough Riders, the J. M. Shaw Rifles, the Houston Cavalry and, of course, the Galveston Sharpshooters.

enemies among the workers they were forced to impress into the burning and clearing details than they did among Fayling's scratch force of volunteers and the hundred and fifty special deputy sheriffs who had been put into the streets shortly before the organized militia arrived. Scurry's *aide de camp*, Colonel Hunt McCaleb, issued orders that anybody found on the streets of Galveston carrying arms who could not show written authority to bear weapons would be placed under arrest, stripped of arms and escorted to jail. Special targets for the duty-minded military police were the special deputies whose only uniforms were big hats and sixguns, whose only authority were hastily made cardboard badges fluttering with ribbons, like those awarded prize steers at fat stock shows. The militia hooted at the badges, relieved the deputies of their revolvers and marched them off to jail. Sheriff Thomas was understandably apoplectic over the high-handed treatment handed out to his men, and it was only after a heated conference between the bigwigs of the city and the military authorities that the affair was straightened out. It was agreed that the civilians could keep their badges and guns, and would patrol the streets during the daylight hours, leaving the hours of darkness to the militiamen.

Major Fayling, who had been seen "falling from the saddle from faintness caused by lack of food and sleep," handed in his resignation to General Scurry. "Sir," he had written, "having been on active service without sleep or food since last Saturday night, 8th inst., I beg to be relieved of my present commission until I can rest and become fit for some duty in the work of relief . . . any kind of duty that may be of use." Scurry thanked Fayling for his "worthy service," and added, ambiguously, that he "cheerfully" relieved him from duty. Red-eyed and grimy, Fayling staggered off to bed.

With the steamer *Lawrence* and the tug *Juno* moving back and forth between Houston and Galveston carrying provisions and volunteer medical workers and street cleaners, Scurry was able to evacuate more than six hundred women and children to Houston, where dormitory space and private housing were thrown open free of charge. Around-the-clock labor got the pumping station repaired; partial electrical power was restored, allowing many of the streets to be lighted; and new cable shipped from Chicago was laid under the bay to restore telegraph service. A heartening sign of normal street life was greeted with cheers on Saturday afternoon, September 15, when conductor R. H. Barrow yelled "Giddap!" to a mule named Lazy Lil, and Car 66 started down the tracks along Market Street carrying passengers in the first revival of public transportation in a week. Plodding between tracks still overlaid with slime and not completely free of sand, Lazy Lil managed to cover a hundred fifty blocks in a single afternoon.

Tents were set up with military precision near the beaches at the western end of town—tents with wooden flooring—and shielded laterines were dug in the sand. Most of those who had been living squatter fashion in the ruins of homes —their own or others', houses without roofs or leaning like the Tower of Pisa—moved into the gypsy encampment provided by the U.S. Army.

But it was like living on a battlefield. The fuel-oil smoke hung over the city night and day, and the heavy air was never free of the smell of carbolic acid, of lime, of putrefaction. Missing were the aerial scavengers, buzzards, "just," as one realistic citizen commented, "when they are most needed." The lower end of the island was a popular haunt for hundreds of these kites, and on clear sunny days they could be seen in great numbers wheeling effortlessly against the sky, riding the rising thermals off the white sands below. But the day following the storm the sky was clear of those wide black wings, and it wasn't until many weeks later that the colony reappeared.

George and Ike Jalonick urged their horses on across the sand. Behind them they towed a small wagon stacked with roughly made coffins, four in all, two of them quite small. The sun blazed down and they shaded their eyes against the glare, peering across the white sand, and seeing a sprawled and bloated form in the distance they trotted forward. The corpse was that of no one they knew and they moved on. The Jalonicks were from Dallas and had come to Galveston seeking the third brother, Ed, his wife and two small children. Ed's wife had prevailed upon her husband to rent a house on the island, preferably near the Gulf breezes, where she and the children could stay until mid-September to escape the brutal inland heat. Ed Jalonick located a house on the isolated western end of town and left his family there while he went back to Dallas. He had returned to Galveston on Saturday to pick up his family, and it was in the house beside the sea that the storm found them all.

George and Ike Jalonick had ridden to the house first, but not even the flimsy foundations remained. There was no sign that a house had ever stood there. They wandered back and forth across the island for three straight days, dragging the coffins behind them, riding as far as six miles to the west, poking at and gingerly examining what remained of more than 150 men, women, and children. They were methodically racing the burning squads. At noon Thursday they found Ed Jalonick in the sand, identified by a laundry mark in the collar of a familiar blue shirt. He was put in a box and a shallow grave dug. Three hours later they were able to fill one of the small boxes with what was left of their nephew, and this was taken back and buried next to the father. Then they started off once again, seeking the other two, hoping their good luck would continue so that the entire family could at some future date be taken back to Dallas.

The Jalonicks, whether or not they succeeded completely in their sad search, were luckier than most. One man who had been prowling the ruins for days looking for the body of his wife came across it in a stagnant pool of water at 33rd Street and Avenue O at the same time as did a squad of Scurry's troops. A volunteer worker named Fernandez watched as "the husband protested and rushed wildly to take possession of the remains. He was practically demented, and the soldiers had to bind him while her body was thrown into the flames."

To those fortunate enough—and they so considered themselves—to discover the bodies of loved ones before the squads did, stealth was required to avoid the hated anonymity of disposal. One Galveston mother, who for obvious reasons wished to keep her name from the authorities, confessed to Mrs. Fannie B. Ward, a relief worker from Washington, D.C., the method she adopted to keep her children from the pyres. Recorded Mrs. Ward: "A widow of considerable wealth lived alone with two daughters, fifteen and seventeen years of age. Their house went to pieces, and both girls were pinned under the walls and drowned. The mother managed to keep their bodies concealed for several days, lest they be cast into the sea or cremated on those ghastly heaps. A friend, also widowed, had lost three small children. The latter brought her precious dead over secretly, one by one; and together, in the darkness of night, the two women dug shallow graves for the five with their own hands and buried them in the dooryard of the demolished home."

So urgent was the need for hasty disposal and so keen was the desire to avoid any taint of looting, that the order was passed to leave the dead unsearched. A worker named Ericson noticed the body of what had been a handsome woman "who had on a fine watch, diamond earrings, several diamond finger rings and gold-clasp garters with her name on them." Ericson called a policeman and pointed out how useful the jewelry would be for identification, but the officer shook his head, and so everything was consumed.

Bodies were found everywhere. Stuck in the ruins of the girders that supported the railroad bridge crossing the bay were forty-eight corpses, scoured and nude, wedged in the steelwork in agonized attitudes. An eighteen-year-old boy named Wagner was found lodged in the forks of a cedar tree two miles from his ruined home, one dead hand gripping two hundred dollars in bills, the other clutching a pair of twenty-dollar gold pieces his father had given him to hold only seconds before the house went down. At Virginia Point, three miles across the bay, one of the nuns from the doomed orphanage was discovered on the beach, nine children still bound to her even in death by the clothesline cut by the workman days before.

The U.S. Marshals generally were effective in keeping sightseers out of the ruined city once they had tightened up the lines of communication leading to the island, but it was impossible to sift out all of the morbidly curious; lurid descriptions of women lying sprawled to the public view dressed only in corsets and shoes led to this believable item in the Dallas *News*, dated September 14: "Word received from Galveston today indicates that Kodak fiends are being shot down like thieves. Two, it is stated, were killed yesterday while taking pictures of nude female bodies. Kodak fiends are notified to stay away." It rings true, except the part about the killing.

By Sunday, September 16, a week after the storm, Scurry's headquarters could report that 40 percent of the lighter debris had been removed from the streets or burned where it stood, and the Galveston *News* had on file the names of two thousand, nine hundred and one missing and presumed dead.

This would run far short of the total, and nobody realized that the recovery and burning of the dead would continue for another five mind-numbing weeks.

# Chapter 10

# RESURRECTION

T HE HURRICANE moved on to the mainland after leaving Galveston and looped across the continent in a reverse S-curve that carried it across eleven states, Nova Scotia and Newfoundland. It returned to the sea, veered north, and finally died in the lonely reaches of the Atlantic east of Greenland twenty days after it was born, a week after laying waste one of America's lushest cities and killing more people than any natural disaster in the nation's history.

On Wednesday, September 12, the storm's vigorous remnants invaded upper New York State after crossing Michigan, Ohio, Illinois, and sweeping up Lake Erie. Buffalo was lashed by 72-m.p.h. winds, and Kingston, Ontario, reported steamers driven aground and the drowning of seamen caught in the open in small craft when gales slammed in from the west during the morning. This destruction from a waning storm gave credence to the reports that had been coming in from Texas, reports that Easterners had until then believed were exaggeration.

But there was no exaggeration.

In Galveston itself, the area of total destruction exceeded 1500 acres, including the denuded eastern end and a stretch of beachfront extending for more than 5000 yards. Here, 2636 houses were knocked to pieces, and elsewhere in town and further down the island another 1000 homes were destroyed, bringing the total to 3636. And the dead. Approximately 3000 corpses were pulled from the wreckage or burned among the debris in the demolished areas east and along the beachfront. Another thousand were strewn in the streets and the yards; 500 were gathered on the shores of the west and north bay areas, and it was guessed that something like 500 were swept out to sea during the few furious hours when the mountains of water crashed against the town. West of town, along the slender finger of sand pointing westward for almost thirty miles, an estimated 1200 were killed out of a total population of 1600. The total killed, then, on Galveston Island reached more than 6000, or nearly 18 percent of the population. Estimates of property damage finally reached $30 million.

When the hurricane smashed inland it crushed small towns along the coast and in south-central Texas in a swath sixty miles wide for a distance of nearly a hundred miles before its energy began to fade. At Velasco, forty miles down the coast from Galveston, 75 percent of the homes were destroyed and four people killed; at Hitchcock, twelve miles north of Galveston, only ten homes out of a total of three hundred were left standing, and thirty-eight people drowned or were killed by falling timbers; at tiny Seabrooke, facing Galveston Bay, thirty-three out of thirty-four homes were destroyed, and twenty-one people died. In Houston itself, only six were killed, but property damage was excessive. Missing and known dead outside of Galveston were estimated to number a thousand.

The precise casualty figure has never been arrived at, and there is hardly any way it could be; but any way the figures are totaled the sum does not drop below 7200 dead. Two months after the hurricane struck Galveston, a list of known dead was published. There are 4293 persons accounted for on this list. The discrepancy between the number of people on the list and the much higher estimate of more than six thousand was explained "on the theory that many neighborhoods were destroyed and no immediate friends were left to furnish names. Moreover, many strangers were in the city for whom there could be no local enquiry, and . . . at the time of the storm many laborers with families had just arrived to work along the docks, and these had no acquaintances. Moreover, it was not always possible to learn the precise number of a family."

The coastal plain was an open-air graveyard for the state's agrarian economy. More than ten thousand head of cattle were killed, and whole counties stank of their carcasses. The cotton crops along the rich bottomlands were in ruins. The rain had torn the cotton and the seed from the fat bolls and the winds scattered the plants for miles. More than fifty thousand bales, worth some $3 million, would never see market.

The calamity drew the attention of the world. From Stettin, Germany's Kaiser Wilhelm II cabled to President William

McKinley, "I mourn with you and the people of the United States over the terrible loss of life and property, but the magnitude of the disaster is equaled by the indomitable spirit of the citizens of the New World who, in their long and continued struggle with the adverse forces of nature, have proved themselves to be victorious. I sincerely hope that Galveston will rise again to new prosperity."

Emile Loubet, President of the Third Republic, cabled from Rambouillet, "It is natural that France should participate in the sadness, as well as in the joy, of the American people. I take it to heart to send to the families of the victims the expression of our afflicted sympathy." From England, Sir Thomas Lipton, the famous yachtsman, cabled his expression of anguish, backed by his personal check for $1000 to help feed the hungry and clothe the naked.

Spontaneous donations rolled in from at home and abroad. Americans living in Paris raised $10,000 and sent it to Governor Sayers; the far smaller American colony living in Berlin collected 2000 marks and dispatched the currency equivalent to Texas. States, cities, fraternal organizations, and individuals swelled the relief fund to nearly $2 million within less than a month. Two little girls in Baltimore opened a lemonade stand, and at the end of the day had collected $1.50 for Galveston. New York City donated a quarter of a million dollars, Omaha sent $3532, and a classic little old lady doddered into a Philadelphia precinct station and told the desk sergeant to mail her dollar bill, the only one she possessed, to Texas. In Washington, D.C., a benefit baseball game was played, and yet another casualty was indirectly added to the hurricane's toll when a batter was hit by a beanball and died four days later in the hospital. The Merchants' Association of New York raised $70,000 and obtained free charter from the Federal Government to use the transport ship *McPherson* for shipping supplies bought with the money. With part of the docks back in operation, Galveston was able to off-load 2000 barrels of flour, 10,000 bags of charcoal, 3000 gasoline stoves, 500 barrels of chloride of lime, 200 barrels of carbolic acid, 5000 barrels of cornmeal, 5000 bags of rice, 5000 bags of white beans, 1000 barrels of split peas, 1000 drums of codfish, 750 sacks of roasted Mocha and Java coffee, 25 chests of tea, 100 barrels of granulated sugar, 1000 tins of baking powder, and 1000 pails of lard.

In Chicago, Dr. William L. Crostwait, a visiting general practitioner from Texas, was walking up Michigan Avenue when the excited cries of a newsboy drew his attention to the first news of the disaster at Galveston. The Chicago *American* building was nearby, and Crostwait hurried inside for more details. He was directed to the newsroom on the fourth floor, where he ran into one of William Randolph Hearst's top aides. Hearst happened to come out of his office and the aide introduced him to "the doctor from Texas." The publisher asked Crostwait into his office, and Crostwait wondered what Hearst could possibly want. Crostwait thought of the magnate as "hardheaded, selfish and arrogant . . . and not credited with any large charity."

Hearst fired a series of pertinent questions about the necessities of disaster relief and railroads in that part of the country, then he picked up the desk telephone and called the district manager of the Santa Fe line to issue several orders, and fifteen minutes later Crostwait found himself as Director of Medical Activities of the Hearst Relief Train, with Hearst's check for $50,000 in his hand. Crostwait ordered cots, blankets, portable operating tables and sterilizers rushed to the train. From among a large number of volunteers the doctor chose five surgeons, eleven nurses and four chore boys. They boarded a Pullman car, a half-Pullman, a parlor car, a diner and two baggage cars and set off nonstop for Texas.

After "the fastest train ride of my life," Crostwait stepped off the Hearst Special at Texas City. It was 3 A.M., and he remembered that the light of a full moon bathed the devastation of the town. He could see the fires burning on Galveston island and the dark fragments of the ruined bridges, and he wondered how he would be able to get his staff and the supplies across the bay. Looking around, he saw the hulk of the beached *Kendal Castle*, listing 30 degrees in her bed of mud. One of the orderlies yelled out, "Ship ahoy!" and in response two British sailors made their way to the train and offered to row everybody across the bay for only twenty dollars. Thus Crostwait was able to spend the first of the Hearst thousands.

A makeshift hospital was set up inside the partially damaged Ball High School near the center of town, and for the next two weeks Crostwait and the others were busy treating fractures and lacerations and making long wagon trips down the island giving aid where needed, dispensing groceries, and dumping chloride of lime on those who were beyond help.

On the Tuesday following the hurricane, Clara Barton, the venerable President of the American Red Cross, left Washington, D.C., with a dozen aides. Miss Barton and the few ladies in the group were put up in the Tremont Hotel, while the men were given cots in a warehouse provided by John Sealy as Red Cross headquarters. Clara Barton had attended more natural and man-made disasters than any woman in the nation's history, including the Johnstown flood eleven years previously that claimed nearly three thousand lives, but Galveston took her breath, and held it. "No description," she commented, "could adequately serve its purpose." Once the routine feeding and dispensing of clothes were organized, she turned her attention to the mainland, where "The poor farmers walked their desolated fields and wrung their hands."

Miss Barton learned that southern Texas was the prime strawberry producer for Northern markets, but that the year's crop was gone with the wind. But if new plants could somehow be set within two weeks, at least a half-crop could be harvested and the industry saved. Using her immense prestige, Clara Barton managed to see 1½ million new strawberry plants rushed to Texas from Louisiana, North Carolina, Arkansas and Illinois in time to save hundreds of farmers from total ruin, and incidentally to assure early berries at breakfast tables in Philadelphia and Boston.

This spare, angular, woman in her seventies seemed to be wilting under the heat and what she remembered as "the stench of burning flesh that permeated every foot of the city. Who could long withstand it?" she asked. On the morning of September 18 she held, as usual, the early morning staff meeting which she always dominated. In the middle of issuing instructions for the day's work, she faltered, then leaned down to whisper in the ear of her vice-president, Mrs. Ellen Mussey. "Begin talking," she commanded. "I'm going to faint." She sat back in her chair, closed her eyes and lapsed into an erect unconsciousness while Mrs. Mussey carried on. Clara Barton received a doctor's attention for the following three months, but she stayed in Galveston the entire time directing field operations, often doing so while propped up in bed.

One of her aides, Fannie Ward (to whom the wealthy widow had confided about hiding her daughters' bodies for secret burial), was an observer with an eye for detail, and has described the macabre atmosphere that hung over the town more than a month after the storm had come and gone.

"A noticeable feature of Galveston these days is the scarcity of household pets such as cats, dogs and canaries. [But] a parrot was found on top of a wrecked home, drenched and shivering, and cackling feebly, *Polly is a poor bird. Polly feels like a damned fool!*

"They are still taking corpses from under the debris. Thirty yesterday, twenty-three the day before, 270 on another recent day. Of course, identification is no longer possible, and the remains are shoveled into the flames as expeditiously as possible. Something like streets have been cleared where the wreckage is piled, with here and there part of a house turned bottom side up and balanced on the apex of its roof, or lying forlornly on its side. The freaks of the wind are shown in walls blown completely away—but the glass globes on chandeliers inside left untouched; in houses twisted completely around on their foundations so that the back door is now the front; and one house left unscathed while its next-door neighbor, for no apparent reason, has been reduced to kindling.

"With very careful driving, one can thread these streets— if he can endure the horrible odors and the clouds of flies which, disturbed by the passing, swarm noisily inside the carriage. If you care to get out and walk a bit, prudently holding your nose, you come across relics of former homes at every step. Within the space of one-half block I counted the remains of nineteen sewing machines, several pianos, children's hobby horses, desks and trunks rifled of contents, shreds of lace curtains and splintered furniture.

"People hereabouts are not eating any fish these days, unless brought in from distant waters—for obvious reasons. Old seamen tell me that never in the memory of man have sharks been seen so close to shore; having feasted on so many corpses they have become bold and eager. . . ."

Clara Barton and the other Red Cross workers left Galveston in time to be back in Washington for Christmas. She recalled that they were all "pale and ill, and even I, who have resisted the effects of so many climates, needed the help of a steadying hand as I walked to the Pullman waiting to take us away."

It is impossible to kill a city that does not want to die.* Given the material possibility for even a hand-to-mouth existence, it is remarkable how quickly spiritual initiative recovers. Cities exist, after all, because they are centers of profitable commercial enterprise, and in this regard Galveston's wounds were superficial. The primary and most obvious fact was that the island itself was intact; the worst hurricane in the history of the continent had succeeded only in robbing the island of an average of three hundred feet of beachline in a kind of instant erosion, and it was reasoned that if a storm of this magnitude could not demolish the island as a geological reality, then nothing could. As soon as they could decently manage it, officials of the wharf company had men out measuring the depth of the sandbar, wondering fretfully if the storm had filled in the channel,

* Some twentieth-century attempts by man and nature, all failures: San Francisco, Louvain, Coventry, Hamburg, Dresden, Hiroshima, Nagasaki, Agadir.

ruining the town as a deep-water port. The fears were groundless; instead of filling, the channel had deepened to twenty-eight feet. And outside of a few chunks knocked off the top, the expensive and income-assuring jetties were as sound as the day they were built.

Another question raised in the minds of those whose livelihoods and plans for expansion depended upon securing loans, and to those on salary, was whether or not Galveston's disproportionate number of capitalists would pull out and take their heavy money elsewhere. Part of the answer was provided on the Monday morning following the storm when W. L. Moody, Jr., and a gang of men began shoveling sand and shattered glass away from the doors of the bank building so that business could be resumed at the usual hour. His father hastened back to town from Manhattan, where he had been when the storm fell, and lost no time in expressing an attitude that would be echoed by his peers in business.

The Colonel replied to an interviewer, "The future? Galveston will be rebuilt stronger and better than ever before. It is *necessary* to have a city here. Even if the storm had swept the island bare of every human habitation and every structure and left it as barren as it was before civilized man set foot on the place, still men would come here and build a city because a port is demanded at this place. I could liquidate and get out of town about as easily as any man here, but that is not my intention. I have had an architect at work all day preparing for the immediate restoration of the bank building, the compress buildings and my other property. We will be pressing cotton within a week; the [blown-in] walls in the cotton warehouses will be better than the ones before because this time I am having them rebuilt myself by day's work instead of by contract.

"The people of Texas have not lost confidence in Galveston; just today we received bills of lading for 300 bales of cotton shipped to us *since* the hurricane—and I do not expect another one like it will strike at this exact spot again within the next thousand years. If I were in the accident insurance business," Moody concluded, "I would sooner write a policy on a man against storm in Galveston than against accident on the New York railroads."

Among the corporate giants Galveston's continued prosperity depended upon was the mighty Southern Pacific, the West's largest transportation combine. Only the year before, S.P.'s chairman, Collis P. Huntington, had won a bitter conference-table battle with board members who wanted New Orleans, not Galveston, as the chief terminus for Southern Pacific's vast network of rail and steamship carriers. Huntington bought 203 acres of land, including 3300 feet fronting Galveston Bay, and had plans drawn for the construction of nine piers. Two of these piers (the largest was 1400 feet long and could accommodate nine ships in line astern formation) were all but completed, and the first all–Southern Pacific rail-to-ship loading and sailing was scheduled for September 15. It was to have been a day of celebration, and vindication for Huntington's judgment in the $1 million initial investment.

Hardly had the flood waters receded, leaving hundreds of boxcars smashed in the yards, than S.P. reaffirmed its faith in Galveston by announcing that it had already ordered a new two-track steel bridge to be built across the bay, a bridge whose trestle work would be ten feet higher than the one just demolished—just in case.

In any event, no significant capital left the island, and the editor of the *News* wrote to a colleague on the New York

*Herald,* "We were dazed for a day or two, but the dead are at rest, and there is no gloom here now as to the future."

The common working man on the island had never been faced with so many opportunities, shared with an influx of laborers from the mainland who came to replace the dead and those, crushed by personal loss who had sold out for twenty-five cents on the dollar, fleeing to places far from the devouring sea. One had only to pick up the newspaper to discover that it was a seller's market.

"Wanted—Carpenters, laborers, tinners, and bricklayers. Will pay good wages. Apply Ed Ringh, Contractor, 4208 Broadway."

"Wanted—A good cook, man or woman, German preferred. A steady position to right party. . . ."

"Wanted—Twenty-five first class tinners, cornice-makers and slaters; good wages. . . ."

Long lists containing hundreds of items similar to these were seen throughout the weeks following the storm, and so were items that revealed how much people wanted to recover essential parts of their lives.

"Lost—During late storm, a large 3-story chicken coop made of iron spokes and wood; coop shaped half-circle. Finder return to C. D. Holmes, Market Street."

"Lost—During the storm, some 150 head of dairy milch cows and calves, principal brand A. Ten dollars reward for every one returned. B. F. Mott, Broadway."

"Wanted for Adoption—Send names and details of any children orphaned by the storm to Box H, the *News.*"

"Information wanted concerning the following children of Joseph B. Aguilo: Frances, 9 years, tall for her age, slender, dark hair, blue-grey eyes; wore a dark blue cashmere dress with three very large buttons across the front, a

rosary of brown beads linked with silver to which was at-
tached a black wooden crucifix. Baby Joe, aged 4 years,
big, dark eyes, lightish hair down to his neck, clipped
across forehead; wore knee pants with buckles at the knee;
shirt with a pink floriated stripe and a little frieze reefer
overcoat. Any reliable information will be rewarded. . . ."

And this, from a realtor on Tremont Street:

"Notice to the World—J.R. Davies & Co. are now ready for
business. We are cast down but not destroyed. We have lost
everything except our hope and courage. Galveston must
and shall be rebuilt—a grander, greater and more glorious
city than the old. Push, pluck and persistency will do it. Our
precious dead, lost in the 'whelming flood are safe; let us
honor their memory by our loyalty to the living. Now for
business. . . ."

By October 19, Richard Spillane—now cured of eczema—
was able to walk the miles of waterfront and report that
thirty-nine ocean-going ships were ranked in the harbor
picking up cargo. He recognized the *Angola* from Glasgow,
the *Volage* from Rotterdam, the *Maria* from Bilbao, the
*Holywell* from Sunderland, the *Hemisphere*, "who has been
here so often she can find her way in the dark," the Norwegian *Origen*, the Mallory's *Lampassas*, the *Borkum* out
of Bremen . . . "more ships than the eye could take in at a
glance." Spillane's ear registered the sounds of a great port
resurgent with life. "The steam hoist dragging the big bales
aboard, the heave of the jammer as he screws the precious
packages into the smallest possible space in the hold, the
rattle of the hand-truck as the gobbler comes rolling the
bales along to the slings, the rumble of the drays bringing
loads of oilcake, flour and other cargo from car to shipside,

the puffing of the locomotives and the crashing of the cars as they are switched in and out of the great long piers make noise enough to waken the dead; but conmingled with these sounds are the raspings of many hundreds of saws and the sharp crack of hammers telling the story of hundreds of builders who, without interfering with the regiments of wharfmen handling cargoes, are restoring the immense sheds, rebuilding the piers and the wharves where the storm ravaged them, and making better and stronger the whole dockage and wharfage system of the port." To Spillane, it was all "marvelous activity and wonderful rehabilitation."

There were more urgent, if less strident, sounds coming from the other side of the island: the creak and slap of planks being dragged out of piles of wreckage to see what was salvageable, and the steady hissing roar of waves crashing against the chewed and ugly beach. These sounds were a reminder that nothing except long odds stood between the slowly reviving town and another disaster rising out of the sea. Isaac Monroe Cline, despite his crushing emotional burden and physical injuries, had returned to his office on the second day following the storm. He watched the shattered town painfully take shape again through nearly four seasons, but the curving shoreline remained ragged and undefended, reminding Cline of the city's past failures that had contributed to the deaths of his wife and children and those of thousands of others. Cline was among those who spoke with passion and with reason in warning that Galveston would inevitably face future assaults by the sea. With the dreadful lesson of neglect still depressingly evident, surely the city would look to its survival in the years to come. Drastic steps were indeed taken, but Cline did not remain in Galveston long enough to witness the city's transformation. In August, 1901, after receiving a commendation from Washington for his work during the hurricane, Cline was promoted and sent to New Orleans as Chief of the Forecast Center for the Gulf States, where he remained for the following thirty-five years of his life.*

There was no chance of securing funds to build a protective seawall until the city administration was reenergized and the chaotic financial structure shored up with workable plans for eventual solvency. The Galveston Deep Water Committee, made up of fourteen of the town's most powerful citizens, took a harsh view of the city's past administrative years and after many weeks of study published a three-thousand-word document calling for draconian fiscal and legislative action to save the foundering ship that had been the pride of the state.† With almost half of the taxable property wiped out, with a floating debt of $204,974.54, with "factional strife, jealousy and dissension" rampant in the city council, and with an alarming number of disgusted and discouraged property owners adamantly refusing or unable to pay taxes "without sacrificing or abandoning what holdings are left to them, the situation is so desperate that desperate remedies are demanded." The committee report stated bluntly that "It is a question with us of civic life or death."

Members of the Deep Water Committee could point to the case of a native of the town who had risen to some promi-

---

* While in New Orleans, Cline pursued yet another avocation, the collection and restoration of Early American portraits in oil. He later sold the paintings for $25,000, many of which can be seen today in the Mellon collection at the National Gallery in Washington, D.C.
† The committee's broadside was signed by George Sealy, A. J. Walker, Charles Fowler, W. L. Moody, R. Waverly Smith, Leon Blum, W. F. Ladd, Julius Runge, J. D. Skinner, Walter Gresham, B. Adoue, Clarence Ousley, Charles L. Wallis, and Morris Lasker.

nence only to "have my home and all it contained swept away. [On September 8] I was worth $12,000," he said, "but today I do not have ten cents to buy breakfast." The man's lot upon which his house had stood cost him $2500, but he managed to sell it for $50, and to raise money "to get my folks out of Galveston" he sold the vault containing the remains of one of his children, who had died nine years previously, for a fraction of its original $3000 cost.

The committee's study came straight to the point. "Our municipal government, as it has been administered during the past twenty years, is a failure. It is immaterial that the position of Galveston is the most commanding on the continent, and that she is the natural port of entry for all the commerce destined for the great West, and the natural point of export for the grain, wheat and other products of all that vast territory, teeming with wealth and abundance, seeking an outlet to the sea; for, while her commerce increased, the city was becoming less and less a fit place for habitation, and probably had as little to show in the way of public improvements and utilities for the money expended for those purposes as any other community in the United States. Sanitary conditions have been going from bad to worse, until they have become dangerous not only for the people living here, but are a menace to the health of the entire state. When the good of the governed seems to have become the last, instead of the first, consideration of those placed in authority, then," continued the report, "an effort must be made to radically change the entire system."

Proposed was the casting out of mayor and aldermen, to be replaced by three commissioners appointed by the Governor of Texas, while two others were to be elected by qualified voters in the town. The governor would have discretionary power to name one of his appointees as president of the Board of Commissioners. Eligibility requirements were simple: at least twenty-five years of age, a U.S. citizen, and a resident of Galveston for a five-year period prior to appointment. Terms were to run for two years—unless terminated first by the governor for inefficiency. The commissioners were to have authority commensurate with their responsibilities. "The consolidation of power," explained the report, "with its attendant responsibility, is the secret of successful administration." The scheme was put before the state legislature and approved in 1901 almost a year after the great hurricane.*

Even before the new commissioners took office, a citizens' committee was at work at closing the barn door on any future storm-wrought disaster. An act was drafted for the erection of a seawall, submitted to the state legislature, and passed on September 7, 1901. When the new Board of Commissioners took office they hired three well-known engineers, including General H. M. Robert, and an exhaustive survey resulted in a cost estimate of $1½ million for a wall not quite three and a half miles long. General Robert may as well have suggested building a concrete bridge to the moon. The money simply was not there, and Galveston's past history of financial fumbling would count against securing any kind of outside loans, even though the new city government was now in the hands of astute businessmen who were already planning sound measures to retire outstanding debts

---

* The constitutionality of the new charter was soon attacked, and after much controversy and litigation a new charter was drawn and passed on March 30, 1903, removing the governor's powers of appointment and returning to the voters the right to elect all five commissioners. But by then great headway had been gained in straightening out the city's finances and other problems.

and replenish the barren treasury. This engineer-general had more to say.

Of course, Robert pointed out, anything like adequate protection will mean raising the grade of the city on an average of from six to eight feet after the seawall is in place. Say another two million dollars. "All this," said one of the commissioners, "was too great for the mind to even contemplate." Here was a chance for the Federal Government to step in and provide the life-saving ramparts; after all, Washington had spent more than $8 million not too many years ago to build and maintain the famous jetties that protected the town's status as a first-class harbor and the net-after-taxes of the Galveston Wharf Company. Surely money would be flowing in for this other purpose?

Not a cent.

Six months passed, and the question went to the voters of the county regarding a proposed bond issue to get the wall started. Only twenty-two votes were cast against the bond issue, which was a voting record of its kind, and on September 19, 1902, a contract was signed with J. M. O'Rourke and Company that promised completion of the wall within fifteen months. The first great pile, forty-five feet long and seventeen inches in diameter at the base, was hammered into the sand at the foot of 39th Street on October 27.

For the next 471 days, excepting Sundays, Galveston shook with the pounding of pile drivers and the rumble of trains and trucks hauling in material from the mainland: 5200 carloads of crushed granite, 1800 of sand, 1000 of cement, 1600 of piling, 3700 of riprap, and five of steel rods. Under the energetic and methodical supervision of chief engineer George W. Boschke, the wall moved slowly eastward along the beach, curved left at the end of the island, and left again up the channel until it joined with the south jetty at the foot of 8th Street to form the shape of a shepherd's crook 17,593 feet long. The massive concrete base was finished in mid-February, 1904, and although the work had fallen behind schedule, there was no complaint about Boschke's Teutonic thoroughness and insistence upon solid workmanship. The wall, concrete and crushed granite weighing twenty tons per linear foot, measured sixteen feet at the base and curved inward to a width of five feet at the top, which stood seventeen feet above mean low tide. Heavy steel reinforcing rods were planted inside the wall every three feet, and sheet piling had been driven deep into the ground in front of the round piles to prevent undermining. Next, the massive irregular granite blocks, weighing several tons each, were moved into place along the entire length of the wall, extending from the base for a distance of twenty-seven feet toward the water, their function being to break the force of incoming waves before they reached the wall itself. On July 29, 1904, Boschke called the last man off the job and the wall was complete. Had it been done fifteen years previously, as a handful of responsible men had urged, there would have been another five thousand people alive to enjoy the benefits.

The county wall, stopping as it did abruptly at 39th Street, left Fort Crockett naked and unprotected. Although no one wished for another twenty-nine drowned or crushed artillerymen, the citizens of Galveston County who were underwriting 4 percent bonds for forty years to pay for their own survival could be forgiven for their satisfaction at seeing U.S. Government property lying exposed to the mercy of the sea. This condition, however, did not last long. The government finally stirred itself to action, but it wasn't until the summer of 1905, nearly sixty months after the hurricane had nearly wiped out Battery O and all its guns, that the military reservation was protected by a mile-long wall just like the one the civilians had, at a cost of nearly $600,000.

Phase Two of the city's strategy to balk future efforts of the sea to invade involved an engineering tour de force without precedent in American history, and remains one of the conceptual and procedural triumphs of all time. The problem was to compensate for the geological evolution that had created an island with a maximum elevation of 8.7 feet, ranging to a minimum of 4.4 feet south of Broadway; the lowest altitudes of just above 2 feet had been obliterated by the storm and were then all under the water in front of the seawall.

The answer to raising the grade in Galveston meant filling in from the top of the wall and reaching to Broadway so that the elevation at the wall would reach to seventeen feet above sea level, and ten feet at Broadway. This meant that every house, every school, every church, every structure in an area forty blocks long and from two to twenty blocks wide would have to be jacked up and filled under—in some cases, with as much as thirteen feet of fill. The streets, of course, would all be covered over and would need repaving later; water pipes, streetcar tracks and everything else laid down by man would have to be raised even before a start on the filling process began. The cost of actually raising the buildings, it was decided, would have to be borne by the individual owners; even so, the fill operation would cost easily $2 million. Already groaning under the bond indebtedness for the seawall, the community wondered where the money was coming from to finish the job. Financing was worked out on the state level when the legislature passed a series of bills in which, for a thirty-five year period, the state turned back to the city all personal and corporate ad valorem taxes, three-fourths of the occupational taxes and all poll taxes except those that belonged to the public school fund. With the funding intelligently solved, engineers turned their attentions to how to raise an entire city.

A great many contracting firms were contacted throughout the country, but almost all of them threw up their hands in the face of the problem. Finally a firm with offices both in New York and in Düsseldorf, Goedhart and Bates, after mulling and figuring, broached their idea, and contract talks were begun and successfully negotiated.

Because the area behind the seawall was so near to the Gulf bed itself, from where the millions of cubic yards of fill would be extracted, work along that area began in the summer of 1904. Then the revolutionary idea of digging a wide and deep canal was carried into effect; this canal opened a gash in the city along Avenue P, beginning at the sea and extending into the heart of the city. Through the canal flailed huge ocean-going dredges, moving inland like prehistoric saurians and spewing fill on both sides of the monster ditch underneath houses resting precariously on stilt-like jacks. Embankments were raised on both sides of the canal to keep the fill-in-solution from spreading into unprepared sections, and outlets allowed the water to drain back into the Gulf. No vehicular traffic was possible, and pedestrians made their way from one house to another via shaky overhead walkways made of loose planking laid down on trestles. An observer who witnessed these bizarre proceedings commented, "The areas being filled resembled river towns during times of flood, and the inhabitants suffered untold inconveniences, as can be imagined. The hardships were accepted philosophically, however, the individual appreciated the great advantages to rise from these temporary annoyances—and was comforted by the thought that the other fellow would have to go through the same experience later."

The incredible job was not completed until almost six years to the day after it began. In July, 1910, the city of Galveston had been raised to specification and was heavier by ten million cubic yards of sandy gulf flooring. Almost every sign of vegetation south of Broadway had been stripped away, and until the long and expensive business of relandscaping with trees, shrubs, and flower gardens was over, the once-lush city reminded onlookers of certain desert communities in the American West.

Hurricanes came and went following the cataclysmic weekend in 1900; five tropical storms struck at Texas before the seawall and grade-raising operations at Galveston were completed, but all of them hurled their violence farther down the coast, one of them all but wiping out the town of Velasco forty miles south. It wasn't until five years after Galveston had raised and corseted itself that Boschke's Wall was called upon to withstand an ultimate bombardment.

On August 5, 1915, a storm was born not far from the western coast of Africa, and after rushing across the Atlantic it invaded the Caribbean below Cuba and sprinted through the Gulf of Mexico for Texas and Louisiana. It fell upon Galveston on August 16 with winds measured at a steady 92 m.p.h., gusting to 120. A three-masted schooner rode with these winds for a hundred miles, having been snatched up that far out in the Gulf, and was hurled over the seawall to crash down on Fort Crockett. Artillerymen left solid cover and risked their lives to bring in the crew. A new causeway linking the island with the mainland went down in a welter of steel and wood—all except one section, atop which was stalled a two-car interurban trolley filled with passengers frightened out of their wits.

When the storm tide came, survivors of the 1900 storm wondered if that horror was going to be repeated all over again. The mountain of water, in fact, rose above the wall and flooded the resurrected town—but only to a depth of five and six feet, and the wall itself was nowhere broken. When it was over, the casualty count in Louisiana and in Texas stood at 275 killed. Only eight of these were in Galveston.

The bondholders and Boschke's workmen were vindicated in every way.

# AFTERWORD

REMINDERS OF Galveston's days of glory are abundant: the great wharves, the channel leading to the open sea, the miles of beaches, and, above all, the awesome architectural monuments to another age that flank oleandered Broadway, still one of the handsomest and certainly one of the more interesting boulevards in America.

The largest of these turreted mansions of limestone, red sandstone, and granite, the Walter Gresham home, was bought by the Roman Catholic Church in 1923 and is now known as the Bishop's Palace. Although when Nicholas Clayton designed the house in 1886 the cost was estimated at a quarter of a million dollars, the purchase price in this century was only $70,000. Now a museum to its times, the

Palace is open to the public. Ashton Villa, J. M. Brown's Mediterranean showcase and the first all-brick house built in Texas, has now become the El Mina Shrine Temple. There are at least three dozen nineteenth-century homes, churches, and even commercial buildings still standing and maintained well enough to give Galveston a two-star rating on the Michelin historical scale as being "worth a detour." These would include the very early frame houses built by two of the founders, Michael B. Menard and Sam Williams, which have withstood numerous storms and the ravages of time over the past hundred and thirty years. The Williams house, however, was not jacked up high enough during the grade-raising operation and consequently lost almost all of its lower floor—a phenomenon common to the more massive homes on Broadway, where the iron fences are noticeably lower than they should be.

After more than seventy years, the survivors of the great 1900 storm are few. We were fortunate enough to spend a very late evening with Mrs. Mary Moody Northen, who was a child of eight when the hurricane struck Galveston. She remembers clearly the terrified expression on the face of the German servant girl who dashed out of the house in the driving rain and scooped up a handful of the water rapidly filling the backyard, returning to cry, "Oh, it's *salt!*" Ironically, Mrs. Northen's great, multi-storied stone house built on steel foundations is threatened by a particularly pernicious kind of termite, and what fire and flood have failed to accomplish over the years may yet be wrought by insects.

Galveston's preeminence along the Gulf Coast as a shipping center was long ago eclipsed by its once-despised neighbor, the giant Houston. But once Houston had achieved its dream of becoming a salt-water port via the long and deep ship channel reaching out for the sea, this was inevitable. The 1900 storm did not "kill Galveston," as was suggested in later years. In fact, the city grew in population and in the volume of business conducted there, but a narrow island has only so much space for expansion, and this was exhausted relatively early. For mainland Houston, expansion was and is virtually limitless. Thirteen hundred ships a year, on the average, still enter and clear Galveston Harbor, but the current wharf company is publicly owned, tax-exempt, and is no longer known as "the Octopus of the Gulf."

Galveston has grown in other ways, as a banking, insurance and hotel center, and most spectacularly as the South's largest medical research and training center—a fact that was almost not realized when the University of Texas regents grew jittery in mid-September, 1900, and wanted to pull the University's newly organized extension to its school of medicine back to Austin. Calmer heads on the island prevailed.

Boschke's Wall has been extended over the years until today it stretches out of sight ten miles down the island. The perennial Gulf breezes still make the island the state's best retreat from inland heat and humidity, and the beaches swarm. Other than from a helicopter or light aircraft, the best public view obtainable of this old and interesting city and its classic enemy, the sea, is to be had from one of the high balconies of the new hotel that runs out over the Gulf of Mexico on steel piers, looking from a distance like a great white ocean liner trying to nose its way into Galveston over the seawall at the foot of 25th Street. From one of The Flagship's private balconies in a distant room that drops

straight down to the water, about where the original shoreline was, the entire city and much of the island is laid to
view. How white and flat it is, and how vulnerable it looks.

H. M. M.
*San Antonio–Fuenterrabia–Canterbury*

# SOME DEVASTATING TWENTIETH-CENTURY HURRICANES

**T**HIS LIST of tropical storms does not include all of those that have brought death and destruction to the United States, but arbitrarily includes the worst, beginning with the one just covered. The Deaths column contains the figure for the U.S. only. Data from the National Oceanic and Atmospheric Administration, Washington, D.C.

| DATES | AREA | HIGH WINDS (IN M.P.H.) | DEATHS |
|---|---|---|---|
| 1900 Aug. 27– Sept. 15 | Texas | 84; gust, 120+ | 7200, est. |

| DATES | AREA | HIGH WINDS (IN M.P.H.) | DEATHS |
|---|---|---|---|
| 1909 Sept. 14–21 | Louisiana, Mississippi | New Orleans: 53 | 350 |
| 1915 Aug. 5–25 | Texas, Louisiana | Galveston: 92; gust, 120 | 275 |
| 1915 Sept. 22– Oct. 1 | Middle Gulf Coast | Burrwood, La.: 106 | 275 |
| 1919 Sept. 2–15 | Florida, Louisiana, Texas | Sand Key, Fla.: 72 | 287 |
| 1926 Sept. 11–22 | Florida, Alabama | Miami: 96; Miami Beach: gust, 132 | 243 |
| 1928 Sept. 6–20 | Southern Florida | Lake Okeechobee: 75 | 1836 |
| 1935 Aug. 29– Sept. 10 | Southern Florida | Tampa: 86 | 408 |
| 1938 Sept. 10–22 | Long Island, New York, New England | Blue Hill, Mass.: 121; gust, 183 | 600 |
| 1940 Aug. 5–15 | Georgia, the Carolinas | Savannah: 90 | 50 |
| 1944 Sept. 9–16 | North Carolina to New England | Cape Henry, Va.: 134; gust, 150 | 46 |
| 1947 Sept. 4–21 | Florida, Middle Gulf Coast | Hillsboro Light, Fla.: 121; gust, 155 | 51 |

| DATES | AREA | HIGH WINDS (IN M.P.H.) | DEATHS |
|---|---|---|---|
| 1954 Aug. 25–31 Carol | North Carolina to New England | Block Island, R.I.: 100; gust, 135 | 60 |
| 1954 Sept. 2–14 Edna | New Jersey to New England | Block Island, R.I.: 87; Martha's Vineyard, Mass.: gust, 120 | 21 |
| 1954 Oct. 5–18 Hazel | South Carolina to New York | New York City: 113; Wilmington, N.C.: 82 | 95 |
| 1955 Aug. 3–14 Connie | North Carolina | Ft. Macon: 75; gust, 100 | 25 |
| 1955 Aug. 7–21 Diane | North Carolina to New England | New York City: 59; Wilmington, N.C.: 83 | 184 |
| 1957 June 25–28 Audrey | Texas to Alabama | Sabine Pass, Texas: 85; gust, 100 | 390 |
| 1960 Aug. 29–Sept. 13 Donna | Florida to New England | Block Island, R.I.: 95; gust, 130; Ft. Myers, Fla.: 92; Cape Henry, Va.: 80 | 50 |

| DATES | AREA | HIGH WINDS (IN M.P.H.) | DEATHS |
|---|---|---|---|
| 1961 Sept. 3–15 Carla | Texas | Port Lavaca and Mata-gordo: 145; gust, 175 | 46 |
| 1964 Sept. 28–Oct. 5 Hilda | Louisiana | Franklin: 135 | 38 |
| 1965 Aug. 27–Sept. 12 Betsy | Southern Florida, Lou-isiana | Port Sulphur, La.: 136 | 75 |
| 1970 Aug. 3 Celia | Texas | Corpus Christi: 120; gust, 160 | 62 |

NOTE: This list includes only those hurricanes that cost twenty or more lives. There is seldom a direct ratio between a storm's severity, the number of lives lost, and the amount of property damage. Helene, in 1958, for example, brought winds gusting to 150 m.p.h. at Cape Fear, North Carolina, and the damage wrought was placed in Category 7 by the U.S. Weather Bureau, i.e., between $5 and $50 million, yet not one life was reported lost. In 1945, Florida, Georgia, and South Carolina were raked by a monster storm that caused Category 8 damage, $50 to $500 million, but only four people were killed.

# ADMIRAL BEAUFORT'S
# WIND FORCE SCALE

I N 1806, Admiral Sir Francis Beaufort, Royal Navy, published a handy table for sailors and landsmen alike that would aid in arbitrarily determining the strength of winds ashore and at sea. The graduated scale ran from 0 to 12, the latter number indicating winds "which no canvas could stand." The Beaufort Scale was adopted for use on the open sea in 1838, and approved by the International Meteorological Committee in 1874. Efforts to correlate the scale numbers to actual wind velocities were not successful until 1939, and with this addition the original as conceived by Beaufort is in use to this day.

| BEAUFORT NUMBER | VELOCITY (IN M.P.H.) | EFFECTS OBSERVED ON LAND | WEATHER BUREAU TERMS |
|---|---|---|---|
| 0 | Less than 1 | Calm, smoke rises vertically | Light |
| 1 | 1–3 | Wind direction shown by smoke drift, but not by wind vanes | Light |
| 2 | 4–7 | Wind felt on face; leaves rustle; ordinary vane moved by wind | Light |
| 3 | 8–12 | Leaves and twigs in constant motion; wind extends light flag | Gentle |
| 4 | 13–18 | Raises dust, loose paper; small branches are moved | Moderate |
| 5 | 19–24 | Small trees in leaf begin to sway; crested waves form on inland waters | Fresh |
| 6 | 25–31 | Large branches in motion; whistling heard in telegraph wires; umbrellas used with difficulty | Strong |
| 7 | 32–38 | Whole trees in motion; inconvenience felt in walking against wind | Strong |

| BEAUFORT NUMBER | VELOCITY (IN M.P.H.) | EFFECTS OBSERVED ON LAND | WEATHER BUREAU TERMS |
|---|---|---|---|
| 8 | 39–46 | Breaks twigs off trees; generally impedes progress | Gale |
| 9 | 47–54 | Slight structural damage occurs (chimney pots, slates removed) | Gale |
| 10 | 55–63 | Seldom experienced inland; trees uprooted; considerable structural damage | Whole Gale |
| 11 | 64–73 | Very rarely experienced; accompanied by widespread damage | Whole Gale |
| 12 | 74 and above | Very rarely experienced; accompanied by widespread damage | Hurricane |

# SELECTED BIBLIOGRAPHY

## BOOKS

ACHESON, SAM. *35,000 Days in Texas*. The Macmillan Co., New York, 1938.

BARNSTONE, HOWARD. *The Galveston that Was*. The Macmillan Co., New York, 1966. (With photographs by Ezra Stoller and Henri Cartier-Bresson)

CLINE, ISAAC M. *Storms, Floods and Sunshine*. Pelican Publishing Co., New Orleans, 1945.

CROSTWAIT, WILLIAM L., AND FISHER, ERNEST. *The Last Stitch*. J. B. Lippincott Co., New York, 1956.

COULTER, JOHN. *The Complete Story of the Galveston Flood*. United Publishers of America, New York, 1900.

DUNN, GORDON E., AND MILLER, BANNER I. *Atlantic Hurricanes.* Louisiana State University Press, Baton Rouge, 1960.

FAULK, ODIE B. *The Last Years of Spanish Texas.* Mouton & Co., London, 1964.

FISHWICK, MARSHAL W. *Clara Barton.* Silver Burdett Co., Morristown, N.J., 1966.

FORNELL, EARL WESLEY. *The Galveston Era.* University of Texas Press, Austin, 1961.

GREEN, NATHAN. *Story of the Galveston Flood.* R. H. Woodward Co., Baltimore, 1900.

GRIFFIN, S. C. *History of Galveston, Texas.* A. H. Cawston, Galveston, 1931.

GUNTHER, JOHN. *Taken at the Flood.* Harper Bros., New York, 1960.

HALSTEAD, MURAT. *Galveston: Horrors of a Stricken City.* American Publishers Association, Chicago, 1900.

HEGARTY, SISTER MARY LOYOLA. *Serving with Gladness.* Bruce Publishing Co., Houston, 1967.

HOUSTOUN, MRS. E. M. *Yachting in the New World.* Steck-Warlick Co., Austin, 1968. (Originally published in 1845)

KEMPNER, ISAAC H. *Recalled Recollections.* Dallas, 1961. (Privately printed)

LESTER, PAUL. *The Great Galveston Disaster.* Waverly Publishing Co., Chicago, 1900.

LUDLUM, DAVID M. *Early American Hurricanes.* American Meteorological Society, Boston, 1963.

MOODY, W. L. & CO., BANKERS. *Three-Quarters of a Century of Progress.* Galveston, 1941. (Privately printed)

MOORE, HARRY ESTILL. *And the Winds Blew.* University of Texas Press, Austin, 1964.

OUSLEY, CLARENCE. *Galveston in 1900.* William C. Chase, Atlanta, 1900.

SHERIDAN, FRANCIS C. *Galveston Island, a Journal.* University of Texas Press, Austin, 1964.

SIBLEY, MARILYN MCADAMS. *The Port of Houston*. University of Texas Press, Austin, 1968.

ZWEINER, DOUGLAS R., AND DARST, ELISABETH. *A Guide to Historic Galveston*. Houston, 1966.


## PERIODICALS

JOHN W. THOMASON, JR., "Catastrophe in Galveston." *American Mercury*, October, 1938.

JOHN FAY, "The Galveston Tragedy." *Cosmopolitan*, November, 1900.

I. M. CLINE Account. U.S. Weather Bureau, *Monthly Weather Review*, November 16, 1900.

WALTER STEVENS, "The Story of the Galveston Disaster." *Munsey's Magazine*, December, 1900.

MAJ. GEN. A. W. GREELY, "The Galveston Seawall." *National Geographic*, November, 1900.

EDWIN MULLER, "The Galveston Flood." *North American Review*, Winter, 1938.

I. M. CLINE, "Special Report on the Galveston Hurricane." *Scientific American*, October 27, 1900.

J. E. WEEMS, "The Galveston Storm of 1900." *Southwestern Historical Quarterly*, April, 1958.

W. MAURY DARST, "An Account of a Mother to her Daughters." *Southwestern Historical Quarterly*, July, 1969.

JOHN CHAPMAN, "Galveston." *Southwest Review*, Winter, 1930.

SISTER M. FRANCIS, "Yellow Fever and Galveston's Ursulines." *Southwest Review*, Spring, 1958.

RUBY CREDO, WITH Z. BOZAXE, "The Galveston Storm." The Houston *Post, Tempo*, September 8, 1968.

FRANCES HARWOOD, "Colonel Amasa Turner's Reminiscenses of Galveston." *Texas Historical Quarterly*, July, 1889.

W. H. HAGGARD, "Where Hurricanes Begin." *Weatherwise*, October, 1960.

### NEWSPAPERS

Chicago *Daily Tribune.*
Galveston *News.* (In microfilm, June 30–October 10, 1900)
Galveston *Tribune*
Houston *Post*
New York *Journal*
*New York Times*
San Antonio *Express*
Washington *Times*

### OTHER

*Thomas S. Henderson Papers.* Barker Historical Library, University of Texas, Austin.
*Central Relief Committee for Galveston Storm Sufferers.* Manuscript, Barker Historical Library, 73 pp. 1902.
*Red Cross Report of Relief.* Barker Historical Library, 95 pp. 1900–1901.
CRY, GEORGE W. *Tropical Cyclones of the North Atlantic Ocean: Tracks and Frequencies of Hurricanes and Tropical Storms from 1871–1963.* Technical Paper No. 55, U.S. Weather Bureau, 1965.
LEE, HARRIS D. *Characteristics of the Hurricane Storm Surge.* Technical Paper No. 48, U.S. Weather Bureau, 1963.

# NOTES AND ACKNOWLEDGMENTS

T HE FOREGOING bibliography cites only those works con-
sulted by the author in preparing this book. In perusing
the volumes published immediately after the storm, the reader
is cautioned to proceed as though he were walking through a
minefield. Halstead's 367-page compilation of "Galveston's horrors," for example, contains a preface dated September 13, 1900,
only five days after the storm, which indicates the haste with
which it was prepared. By far the most reliable contemporary
source is Ousley's *Galveston in 1900,* written as a hedge against
the over-sensational and whose profits were used to help rebuild
Galveston's schools. A source of architectural history, for which
the city became famous, and a sheer visual delight is Barnstone's
large volume, illustrated by two of the world's most perceptive

photographers, Stoller and Cartier-Bresson, whose styles are disparate but by no means conflicting.

For help of all kinds, the author is indebted to the following:

*In Galveston:* Mr. Bob Dalehite, Archivist, Rosenberg Public Library; Miss Sarah Randles, Assistant Archivist; Mr. John Hyatt, Director. Mrs. Mary Moody Northen. Mr. W. L. Moody IV. Mr. John Hamilton. Mr. Tom Purdy, General Manager, Galveston Chamber of Commerce.

*In San Antonio:* Mr. Maury Maverick, Jr. Miss Barbara Ettinger, San Antonio Public Library. Capt. Thomas Camp, U.S.A.R. Mr. Edward R. Villastrigo.

*In Austin:* Mr. Lonn Taylor, Barker Historical Library. Mr. Fred Folmer, Librarian, The University of Texas Library.

*In McQueeney, Texas:* Mrs. Marilyn Collins.

*In El Paso:* Mrs. Virginia P. Hoke, Head, Reference, El Paso Public Library.

*In Washington, D.C.:* Mr. Charles G. Thomas, Office of Public Information, ESSA, Weather Bureau. Mr. J.W.G. Stephens, Jr.

*In England:* Capt. Tempest Hay, Royal Navy, Ret., and Mr. Fred Isaacs, both of Mystole Park, near Canterbury.

And to Rigmor, for long hours spent capturing on film the essence of Old Galveston.

976.4                    Cop.1

Mason
  Death from the sea.

        976.4                    Cop.1
                                 $7.95
        Mason
          Death from the sea.

            SEP   9
            MAR  28              37058
            JUN  23          35297
                             52481

AUG     1972